10 COMMANDMENTS
to Ivy League and Stanford

I Core Academic Courses	**VI** SAT II
II GPA	**VII** College Essay
III AP, IB, & Honors	**VIII** Activities
IV AP Exams	**IX** LOR
V SAT I	**X** Interview

Alex Hull, *Harvard, M.Ed.*

Former Harvard Alumnus Interviewer
UC Berkeley Undergraduate Admissions External Reader

1o Commandments to Ivy League and Stanford

2012
First Edition
Printed in the United States of America.

ISBN 978-0-578-10661-8

PREFACE

Today's college admissions process is no longer between accept and reject but rather it involves three processes - accept, reject, and defer. For the 2,017 students placed on the waiting list by U Penn in 2012, the admissions process starts all over again in April to compete for the last few spots that remain. In order to prevent the prolonged agony of getting placed on a wait list, I cannot emphasize enough how important it is to apply 110% of your ability, effort, and talent every day of your high school career. I have seen many seniors and their parents who are ecstatic after receiving acceptance letters. However, I have also seen too many seniors and their parents who are devastated after receiving rejection or deferral letters. One of my students, who was accepted to Harvard, testified during our college seminar that throughout her high school years, she "did everything possible to the point of exhaustion and there were no more stones unturned." I think this statement exemplifies the need for all of you to do your utmost each day.

Today, U.S. colleges are attracting the best and the brightest from all over the world. Higher education in America consists of some of the best institutions of learning in the world. We have renowned scholars, state-of-the-art facilities, and the freedom to expand your experiences and develop your minds beyond all imagination. It is little wonder that we attract a large number of students, particularly from China, India, and Korea. For example, as of December 2008, we had 72,190 active F-1 visa students from China. As of December of 2011, this number has increased 173% to 196,857.

This trend has placed extraordinary pressure and stress on American high school students and will continue to do so over the next decade. In addition, we now have a record number of domestic applicants to the nation's top universities. For example, in 2012, Stanford had a 6.6% increase in the number of applications compared to the previous year, breaking the record yet again with

36,631 applications. It is ironic that the high school age population has been decreasing while the number of college applications has been increasing. This may be attributed to the fact that the average number of college applications per student has increased significantly. This trend too will continue as colleges place more and more emphasis on the waiting list in order to increase their yield rates.

So, what is the solution? Legendary management consultant, Peter Drucker said, "Today, knowledge has power. It controls access to opportunity and advancement." If you understand the dynamics of the U.S. college admissions process, you will have less stress and will be able to streamline the road to your dream college without incurring expensive and time-consuming detours.

I wrote this book in an attempt to give back to the next generation by providing a blueprint for college admissions. I hope this book will serve you in your pursuit of lifelong happiness in the following ways. Firstly, it will help verify whether or not you are on the right track. Secondly, it will suggest innovative ideas to better develop your character, dreams, and goals. Lastly, it will motivate and empower you, regardless of your nationality, ethnicity, gender, or financial circumstances. Today, the U.S. college admissions process is no longer accessible without having a well-thought-out, four-year strategic academic plan in addition to keeping up with the latest statistics and information to make periodic adjustments.

I would like to dedicate this book to Jennifer, David, Amanda, Allison, Trevor, and my family. I give thanks to all of my students and teachers who have made this book possible. I especially send my deepest gratitude to all the parents throughout the world who are sacrificing their lives in order to provide better opportunities for the next generation.

Sincerely,

Alex Hull

TABLE OF CONTENTS

PART I: YOUR MISSION AS A STUDENT

PART II: TEN COMMANDMENTS OF COLLEGE ADMISSIONS

PART III: COLLEGE APPLICATION PROCESS

PART IV: CONCLUSION

PART I

YOUR MISSION
AS A STUDENT

1. YOUR PERSONAL COUNSELOR

Do you know what the high school student to counselor ratio is in the U.S.? The national average student to counselor ratio for the 2009-2010 academic year was actually 459 to 1. For California public high schools, the student to counselor ratio is even higher at 810 to 1.[1] In addition, these counselors are often too busy dealing with conflict resolution. As a result, counselors don't have sufficient time to provide adequate academic advice, particularly college counseling. And when they do, some of the advice is outdated because most high school counselors are overworked and underpaid. In other words, your high school counselor may not be compatible for your parents' and your academic goals. I am here to help you through the entire college preparation process from beginning to end, not simply only by getting your SAT scores up or helping you choose extracurricular activities but also by offering you the blueprint to the college of your dreams.

[1] SOURCE: American School Counselor Association, Academic Year 2009 – 2010.

2. WHY DO YOU STUDY?

Why are you reading this book? Because of your parents? Perhaps you feel you need to better prepare yourself for college. Nevertheless, whether you're reading this out of your own volition or through explicit pressure from your parents, you are reading this book. This is not for your parents. So, have a positive attitude! This book is for you.

Think about homework. What is the main difference between homework and studying? Does homework come to an end? Of course! If your homework is to memorize 25 words by next Friday, when you finish memorizing them, you're done. For whom do you do your homework assignments? You do them for your teachers so they can evaluate you. At school, in order to get a letter grade, you need to complete your homework.

On the other hand, what about studying? Does it come to an end? No! Studying never comes

Studying never comes to an end because studying is for YOU!

to an end! Because you can always learn one more word, you can always learn how to read a little faster, you can always learn how to write a little better, or you can always learn how to solve that math problem faster.

For self-improvement, you need to do your homework AND study. So let's say you have to memorize 25 SAT words for tomorrow. What are you going to do next? Move on to the next list. Start working on the next 25 words because you will need to know those words anyway. You might as well look at those words in advance so you can learn them sooner rather than later.

I want you to have this mentality because this is the way college works. High school is all about getting homework done and getting ready for a pop quiz or final exam. But once you begin college, graduate school, medical school, or law school, it is all about obtaining knowledge for yourself so that you can retain more knowledge to move on to bigger and better things in life. So, think ahead.

What is the main difference between you and the students who received a perfect 2400 score on the SAT? I've been teaching the SAT for the past 24 years now, and I can confidently tell you that the SAT has very little to do with intelligence. It is not an IQ test. If it were, they would have called it SIQ. This test is all about effort! The SAT is an assessment test to find out your ability in critical reading, math, and writing. So what is the difference between you and the students who've finished taking the SAT? They learned all these skills yesterday and you are going to learn them TODAY or TOMORROW. That is the only difference.

Remember, no one was born with a rich knowledge of vocabulary in their head. Can you imagine? A little infant spitting out SAT words, running around the hospital? No way. That doesn't happen. Just as you, I had to learn one word at a time. Oftentimes I forgot the words so I had to look them up over and over again, ten, twenty times until they finally clicked. Memorizing vocabulary takes time and effort. Got it? Here's the good news. I learned them yesterday; you will learn them today and tomorrow. In the end, we will be equal.

3. HOW BADLY DO YOU WANT THAT COLLEGE?

In the end, this is all about EFFORT. If I ask you right now to do 100 pushups, most of you will go, "Say what? You're kidding me." and you'll probably get sick of trying and give up at a certain point. But if you build up strength by doing 30 pushups today and 40 pushups next week, some of you might come back awed and say, "I can do 100 pushups now." Do you see what I'm getting at? Before you couldn't even dream of doing 100 pushups but through effort, perseverance, and practice, you could reach the goal. Eventually, you would get up to 100. It may take six months, it may take a year. But for some people it may just take only a week. Why? Because they want it more.

I'll give you an example. Remember the presidential fitness award— the little blue patch with an American eagle on it? When I was growing up it was a big deal! Everybody wanted that patch, and if you didn't get the blue one, you got the next level red patch. Remember? There are certain  fitness requirements you have to fulfill to receive the award, for instance, one mile run, pull-ups, shuttle runs, sit-ups, etc. Well, when I was in 7th grade at Jefferson Junior High School in Long Beach, I was able to do everything except nine pull-ups. I don't know what the standard is now but back then, I needed to do nine pull-ups to get the presidential patch. I could do only three. It killed me. Luckily, my coach, Mr. Anderson gave me one more week to do nine pull-ups. Do you know what I did that week? I went home and every chance I got I did pushups to strengthen my arms. My dad used to own a grocery store on 15th Street, and I intentionally grabbed two to three cases of soda pops and carried them to different locations over and over

13

again, so that I could increase arm strength. One week later, it was the day for my second chance to do nine pull-ups.

One, two, three, four...

I'm thinking, 'Yeah, halfway there.'

Five, six, Se—ven...

Everybody's looking at me and cheering me on, "Go Alex!"

Eight!

I'm dying, but oh my gosh!

Just one more.

I'm barely coming up.

My arms are shaking.

My body is shaking.

I just barely pull my chin over the bar.

NINE!

YES! NINE!

I DID IT!!!

Do you know how good I felt? If you've accomplished a goal in the past you know what I'm talking about. It feels great. All that hard work paid off. And I was able to get that presidential award. You might be thinking that's no big deal, it's just a blue patch, whoopee-doo, right? But that was one of the happiest days of my life.

What did I learn from this experience? In this world, if you want it badly enough, you can get it. You say to yourself, "I want to be a doctor, I want to be a lawyer, I want to be a CEO, I want to be an engineer, I want to be a successful venture capitalist." You know what? If you want it badly enough, apply yourself, and focus on what you have to do for each step, then, you can achieve it.

4. APPLY YOURSELF 100%

I came to the U.S. when I was eleven years old. In 1971, my father moved to the U.S. with a mere $300 in his pocket. In 1973, our family followed him to Los Angeles. My father had purchased Tokyo Café, a small hamburger shop near the corner of Manchester and Vermon in Inglewood, California. The day after I arrived, I started working as a dishwasher and waiter in this shop. The first English words I learned were HB (hamburger) and CB (cheeseburger). I still remember the HB combo was 69 cents. When I was thirteen years old, we saved a little money and moved to Long Beach. My parents bought a "mom and pop" grocery store in Long Beach, where poverty and crime rates were high, and named the store, "15th Street Market." Every day after school, I would bike ten blocks from home to the store to bring dinner to my parents and uncle. I used to stock merchandise and keep an eye open for shoplifters. Each sunset, I would go outside to be on the lookout for suspicious people.

One night while keeping a lookout, I got thirsty. So I came into the store, grabbed a can of Coke, and took a gulp. As soon as I turned around, a large tall African American man pulled out a 22-caliber handgun and pointed it directly at me. I was only thirteen years old. I can still vividly remember seeing the bullets in the barrel merely two feet across from the counter. I looked down to avoid making eye contact with the guy. My dad was standing in front of the cash register next to me. My mother was sitting behind my dad counting coins and putting them into a paper roll. I can still remember the incident like it was yesterday. My dad pulled out all the cash from the cash register and gave it to the robber. My dad asked, "Do you want the coins too, buddy?" The man said, "No." He grabbed the cash, and said, "If you call the cops or move in the next thirty minutes, we will come back and shoot every one of you!" I was scared. The whole incident took maybe three minutes, but it felt like an eternity. I felt so helpless. There was nothing I could do. I didn't know what the man was going to do next. All he had to do was to pull his finger a quarter inch on that trigger and I would have been killed. My dad and mom would have been dead or injured too. Who knows? My whole life flashed before me. All of this was going through my mind when he was pointing the gun at me. Thank God no one was injured but I had nightmares for years. But, you know what? That turned out to be one of the best days of my life!

Yes! Because from that day on I said, "In this country, I could die tomorrow." There were so many things I had yet to do in my life: traveling to Europe, falling in love, driving a sports car. So at that moment, I made up my mind! I said, "From now on, I'm going to apply 100% of my God-given talent to everything I do, whether it is school, sports, or just having fun. I'm going to go for it. I am going to live each day to the fullest!" And that's how I've been living my life since. Once I started doing that, everything began to click; everything began to fall into place. I started getting better grades. I started becoming good at sports, so eventually I became captain of my varsity soccer team as a junior in high school. I worked hard but I played hard too. What if there's no tomorrow? What if there's no next year? How sad would that be, not having been able to enjoy many things that you wanted in this life?

5. THE SECRET FORMULA TO BETTER GRADES

 Let me ask you a question. Are you happy with the grades that you received last semester? If yes, awesome! If not, why not? Do you know how to get better grades in school? I have a secret formula. Here it is.

Spend more time!

It's that simple. Are you having a hard time with Spanish? That's because you're not spending enough time on it. So, you're behind; therefore, you don't understand your irregular conjugations; so, it's frustrating; therefore, you hate it; now, you hate the Spanish teacher. See how it works? On the other hand, you like math, you get good at it because you spend more time on math. When you take a quiz, you get a good grade. A good grade makes you happy. Now you want to spend even more time on math, and yes, you love your math teacher.

AP U.S. History is probably the most demanding class in high school because there's so much reading and writing you have to do. Spend some time on it during the summer before and you'll have less stress during the course. You'll be one of the few students who will get an A in that class. However, you have to compromise. You have to give up something; YouTube, Facebook, computer games, iPod, texting,

shopping, TV, just horsing around, hanging out… You get the picture? Whatever it is, you have to compromise those hours and sacrifice. Why? Because if you don't, you might miss the opportunity to reach your maximum potential, attend the college of your choice, and live your life to the fullest.

6. SET YOUR PRIORITIES

There's a difference between knowing the subject matter versus getting an A in class. I mean, I studied my brains out before, and I took the test and I received a C. What happened? I just studied so hard! I don't get it. This is not fair. How many of you have gone through this experience? Then, there's this clown sitting in

the back of the classroom who never seems to do anything and yet somehow gets an A (without cheating) and you go, "Man, what's up with that?" Life is not fair! Yes, there's a difference between knowing the subject matter versus getting a good grade in class. 'A' students understand this concept.

School should be all about knowledge and learning. But in our education system today, it's all about grades and test scores. It sucks; it shouldn't be that way. But here is a reality check: unless you get good grades and scores, you will have a difficult time getting into a good college. So set priorities for yourself and make the sacrifices. Why? If you do <u>NOT</u> make the sacrifices, you will kick yourself come senior year. Now, I am not saying that you have to study 24 hours a day. I just mean that you have to set priorities. Take care of your business first as a student, then play.

You know what it is… While you're playing Call of Duty: Modern Warfare 3, in the back of your mind you're going, "Man, I've got to do that chemistry homework." You feel guilty. Right? I've been there. When you're playing games or on Facebook, you think, "I've got to study," and you feel guilty. So take care of homework first and then play. You'll feel better and you will enjoy yourself more. You won't have anything more to do. You can relax. You'll be less stressed. You'll be happier. Therefore, manage your time better and do <u>NOT</u> procrastinate.

7. YOUR JOB AS A STUDENT

Did you know you have a job? What is your job title? Your job is being a student. Your job description is to go to school and get the highest grades possible without cheating. Did you know that you get paid to be a student? Do you pay rent? No. Do you pay for breakfast, lunch and dinner? No. You get sick. Who pays for the medical bill? You need money to see a movie. Who pays for your ticket? Your parents! You are a professional student and you get paid to be a student. It's probably the best job in the world. Why? You'll never get fired. So what's your job? Your occupation is a STUDENT.

Monday through Friday, you are supposed to put in eight hours a day, full time. You go to school from what? Eight to three? Minus lunch and break time, so you are spending six to seven hours at school. Then, you study two to four hours after school and do your homework. Now, what if you can't study after school because you get sick or because you have to go to a birthday party, what now? You have to make up the time or put in overtime. If you don't finish by Friday night, you may have to put in six or seven days that week. You may have to work Saturday and Sunday. So, Saturday and Sunday are your period to catch up on those things you couldn't do during the weekdays. If that's not enough, you shouldn't go to that birthday party or ski trip. Learn to set your priorities and say, "Mom, Dad, I'd love to go but I've got to stay and study. I need to take care of my business first." If that's not enough, you've got to spend summer or winter vacation catching up. Do you follow? That's what you need to do now. Not because your mom or dad asks you to or makes you do it. Those days are gone. You're not a little kid anymore. If you're still doing that, you must change. Why? Because this is all about you and your life. If you mess up now, you are going to pay for it later.

8. WHAT KIND OF JOB DO YOU WANT?

So why are you here? Many of you are still reading this book because you want to do your best in high school, and get the highest possible SAT or ACT score, so that you can significantly increase your chances of getting into the college of your choice. Now, why is that important? Getting into college is only the first step towards having a happy life. Don't you want to be happy? Don't you want to laugh and say, "My goodness, I love my life so much. It's worth living." Don't you want to have the luxury of helping the less fortunate people who are struggling? Don't you want to make a difference in this world for the next generation?

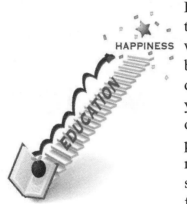

Education is the stepping stone towards having a happy life, whatever that happiness may be. People may have different definitions of happiness. What is your definition? To me, education opens up doors. Movie stars or professional athletes may not need college and education to be successful. But they're far and few between.

So let's define our reasons for sacrificing our evenings and weekends so that we can be happy ten, twenty, or thirty years from now. Each day I see thousands of people sitting in traffic on the freeway at 5:30 pm. Imagine you had to do this Monday through Friday? What about in the morning? You have to get up at 6 am. Drop off your kids. Fight traffic to get to work by 9 am in the morning each day.

There are two types of jobs in the world. The first type of job is, "Man, I hate this job. It sucks. I can't stand my boss. He's such a jerk. I can't stand my coworkers. They show no respect. But I've got to feed my family. I've got to take care of my kids. I've got to pay the mortgage. I don't have a choice." What's the second type of job? "Man, I love this job. I can't believe they're paying me to do this job. I look forward to going to work. I don't mind staying until six, seven or even later at night. I don't mind working Saturdays and Sundays because this is my passion. It makes me happy to work."

Joanna Coles, Editor-in-Chief of Marie Claire Fashion Magazine and Adweek's Editor of the Year in 2011 says it best, "I never wake up in the morning thinking, 'Ugh, I have to go to work!' It's always, 'Oh! I can't wait to get there!"

I L♥VE MY JOB

I would like you to consider having a job that would make you HAPPY. First generation Americans like my parents had little choice. Do you think our parents loved being dry cleaner owners? "Oh, yes I love it. 90 degrees outside, I'm ironing a shirt so it feels like120 degrees. I can't turn on the air conditioner so I've got to turn on the fan. What do I make? $1.25 a shirt, but after tax and rent, maybe 35 cents a shirt?" No way. They did not enjoy their jobs but they had no choice. Or a convenience store owner? Dealing with all those irate drunks or minors who want beer or cigarettes? You've got to deal with them seven days a week. I know what that is like because my parents owned a grocery shop for twenty-two years. They left the house at 6:30 am to open up the store by 7 am seven days a week. They returned home after midnight. Many times my two brothers and I didn't see our parents for days because they came home after we went to bed at night, and they left the house before we woke up in the morning. After school, we came home and bought fast food or ate ramen. No mom or dad to take care of us. That's the way I grew up.

Choose the job that you like, something that you are passionate about, the job that will make you happy; the job that makes a difference. Don't get the job that you have to go to because you need to pay the mortgage and take care of your family. When I was growing up my folks could never come to my games or school events. They never met with my teachers during open house because they didn't have time. So, I promised myself, "When I grow up, I'm not going to do that. I'm going to be there for my kids." This was a choice I made as a child. You too will have that choice. Twenty, thirty years from now, when you're thirty-something or forty-something, what type of job will you want? How many days a week will you want to work? Seven days? Five days? Four days? Or whenever you want? Where do you want to live? What kind of car do you want to drive? How many kids would you like to have? Do you want to go to Hawaii every summer? Don't you want to enjoy your life and life earnings rather than stress about work, work, work all the time?

I INCREASE MY CHANCES OF BEING HAPPY SIGNIFICANTLY BY GOING TO A GOOD COLLEGE.

9. BE A GREAT STUDENT

Have a dream. Have a target. Set a goal. Because once you establish your goal, the process is easy. Then you start to realize, "Ah, I see. That's why I have to go to a good graduate school. I see. That's why I have to do well in college. I see. I've got to do really well now in high school. I see. I need to do better in 10th grade." It makes sense because it's a linear process. See a sample below.

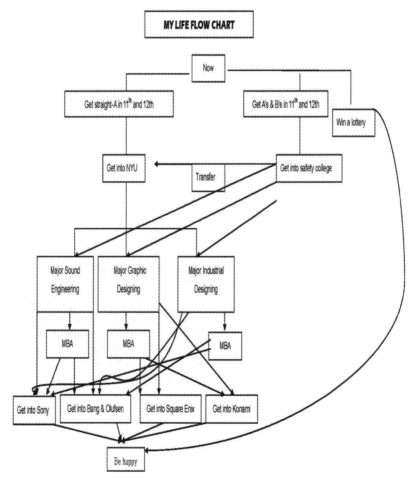

If you don't have a goal, you don't know why you're going to school now. You study, but  you don't know why you're doing it. You do it for the wrong reason. Are you trying because of your mom or dad? So they can have bragging rights when you get accepted to a top college? So they can call up their friends or relatives and say, "Oh, hi, Mrs. Lee. My daughter just got into Stanford. How about your kid?" Is that why you're doing this? No, it's not about that. Money? Maybe some of you say, "I want to make lots of money. I want to go to a good college." Think again. If you chase money, money flies away.

But if you're passionate about something, like Bill Gates, you're going to make a ton of money. Do you think Bill Gates, with his buddies when he started designing these software programs, said, "Oh man, we're going to be billionaires when we create this software"? No way. They were so consumed with their passion; they could care less about anything else. Now, look at them. Money came because they were passionate about their job and devoted 100% of their effort.

Some of you already know what you want in life. Others don't know what you want yet and that's OK because that's what college is for. For example, you take psychology classes in college and you go, "Wow! This is really interesting. I like this. You know what? I want to be a psychologist." That's what college can do for you. You explore different fields, so that you figure out what you want to do for the rest of your life to become a productive member of our society and be happy. Then, money will come. Because if you're passionate about something, people will recognize it and money will follow.

Now, it's how you use the money that makes you an altruistic person versus a selfish person. It's not about the mansion and Porsche because that's never enough. Your mansion will never be big enough. I want a bigger house. The Porsche is never fast enough. I want a faster car. One is not enough. Two, three, it never ends.

But if you earn money to take care of yourself and family, and to help less fortunate people, that is the true purpose of education. Education is about *non sibi*, a Latin phrase meaning "not for self." When you look at the motto of Phillips Academy, a prestigious high school in Massachusetts, you will see the phrase *non sibi*. Education is not about your own enrichment; education is all about how you can improve your God-given talent to help people in our community, state, country, and world.

So, I don't care what you did yesterday. Let's start clean. Wipe everything off the table and start fresh. I want you to rearrange the furniture if need be, pull down all those sports and music posters, put up SAT words, a Chemistry element chart, and Spanish irregular conjugations. Make your room into a study room. Not because mom or dad tells you to, but because you want to.

10. ORGANIZE YOUR SCHEDULE

We are creatures of habit. Without a clock, you could be anywhere in the world, at a certain time of the day, and you will get hungry because you are used to eating food at that particular time. How many of you have gone to another country in a different time zone? You get up in the middle of the night because you are hungry. Why? Because you are used to eating at that particular time while you were in the U.S. Your biological clock recognizes mealtime even though the clock is set to a different time zone. What is my point? When we have a set time to study every day, our body will recognize it. I would like you to block out three or four hours of your day and dedicate it to studying and doing homework.

Let me give you some tips. Some of you may be a morning person like I am. No matter what time I go to bed at night, I wake up at the crack of dawn at 5 am. Maybe I became used to this because my grandmother reared me when I was a kid. My mother was a business woman, and she was out there working so she said, "Mom, take care of my son." My grandmother always woke up early so I'd wake up with her. By around ten or eleven o'clock at night, I am dead tired. I am ready to hit the sack. I remember when my brothers and I were in high school and college and we would go out to parties. Ten o'clock came and I went, "Yawn, I've got to go to bed." And I would say, "Paul! Ray! Let's go home, I'm tired," and they would say, "You party pooper! The party's just getting started." So for me, staying up and studying at ten or eleven o'clock is a bad idea. I can't stay awake. Are you like me or my brothers?

How many of you play sports after school? When I was playing sports during high school, for away games I would come home at seven or sometimes eight o'clock at night because of traffic jams. When I did get home, the first thing I did was eat. Boys don't take showers, we eat first. What happened after that? I got drowsy. I could barely finish my homework and would fall asleep. I could not keep up. What I ended up doing was playing catch up throughout the whole year. So I said, "Enough of this." After I ate, I would go to bed at 9 o'clock. Then, I would get up at two or three in the morning and study. Now, how many people have stayed up until two or three in the morning to study? What is it like? It's quiet. Your mom is not looking over your shoulder saying, "What are you doing?" Your dad isn't walking around. No little brother or little sister who wants to talk to you. It's quiet. So I was able to concentrate and focus for three or four hours straight and take a little nap on Sundays or Saturdays to catch up on my sleep. I am not recommending all of you do this, but for me as a morning person it worked!

Now, some of you, like my brothers, are night people. I remember when we were young and living in Orange County, we had this major 6.5 earthquake in the early morning hours. I was shaken awake from bed - the whole house was shaking - so I ran to my brothers' rooms and said, "You guys! Get up! Earthquake!" and they were going, "ZZZ," just snoring away. They slept right through this major earthquake. That's how bad they were in the morning. If they had it their way, they would sleep until 1 o'clock in the afternoon. You know the type. For them, trying to get up early in the morning to study? Forget it. It's not going to happen. But they could stay up all night to study. So for people like my brothers nighttime is the best time to study.

You need to identify when you are at your peak. For some people, it might be right after school, 3 pm, everything's fresh in your mind, just as my daughters. They come home, they do their homework, and they're done. For other people, it might be after dinner or really late at night. Whichever type you are, I would like you to block out three to four hours a day Monday through Friday, so you do this routinely.

How many people work out or jog every day? What happens when you can't do it one day? How do you feel? You don't feel right. You feel sluggish. It feels like you missed something. That's the feeling I want you to get when you miss studying. But it has to be routine because we all know what usually happens. You sit down to study and your friend calls and says, "Dude, let's play some basketball." It's a nice day out, it's been raining for a few days, so you say, "Ok. Sure." You go out there and start playing basketball. What are you thinking? "Oh man, I've got to do that homework. It's bugging me. I've got a chemistry exam coming up, I should study." Throughout the whole time you're playing, all you're thinking about is that chemistry exam. Don't do that! **Take care of your business first.** Now you're free and relaxed to play, treat yourself, go shopping, or do whatever you want to do for the next few hours.

11. REVERSE ENGINEERING

Why do well in high school? To truly understand what universities are looking for you need to look at the blueprint first. Most colleges use the Common Application. As of 2012, there are 456 colleges on the Common Application member list. Therefore, regardless of your current grade, my advice is to fill out the Common Application as though you are applying to colleges right now. Why are we doing this? To figure out where you are right now as an 8th, 9th, 10th, or 11th grade student so that you can make improvements before your senior year. Most high school students don't look at the application until their senior year. Rarely do they look at it before they enter the 12th grade. **NOT US!** We're going to do this today, right now! I don't care if you are a freshman or even an 8th grader. By doing this as early as possible, you can see the big picture and also share it with your parents so that they can help guide you. This way, your parents won't fight or resist you but instead work with you as a team, saving money and time.

Filling out the Common Application now shows where you are right now as 8th, 9th, 10th, or 11th grade students in terms of academic courses, extracurricular activities, GPA, SAT, or ACT so that you can make improvements before your senior year.

"It is important to realize that the admissions committee is oftentimes trying to build a cohesive campus community rather than simply selecting the most qualified students. Thus, much of college admissions boils down to being a matching process - are you a good fit for the school and vice versa? Since there are plenty of traditional applicants with stellar grades and strong test scores (which of course, is a pre-requisite to even applying to the top schools), your stats alone won't make you stand out. It helped me to take the time to sit down and critically assess what kind of person I am, what I want out of my four years, and what qualities I can bring to a community. Rather than using a check-off-the-box kind of system in which you try to stack up as many awards, community service hours, leadership positions without a clear direction, first figure out exactly what you want to highlight and plan accordingly."

Anonymous, Yale, Class of 2012

PART II

TEN COMMANDMENTS
OF COLLEGE ADMISSIONS

1. CORE ACADEMIC COURSES

Solid academic courses are the subjects that admissions officers evaluate to see how serious of a student you are. You need to challenge yourself in high school. Try to take the maximum number of courses you have at your high school. This may be different from your high school graduation requirements. Your senior year schedule should be full of Honors and AP courses. In the Common Application School Report, it asks your high school counselor how demanding your course selection was compared to the other students in your school. The admissions officers want to see how strongly you have prepared for college. The courses may be different depending on your high school but I recommend the following subjects and classes for admission to top colleges.

9th Freshman	10th Sophomore	11th Junior	12th Senior
English	English / (H)	English / (H) (AP)	English / (H) (AP)
Fundamentals	American Literature	European Literature	Literature / Composition
Geometry	Algebra II / Trigonometry (H)	Pre-Calculus / Math Analysis (H)	Calculus AB/BC / Statistics (AP)
Biology or Science (Lab)*	Chemistry (H/AP)*	Biology/Physics (AP)*	Physics/Anatomy (AP)*
Western Civilization	World History (AP) or European (H)/(AP)	U.S. History (H)/(AP)	U.S. Gov't / Econ. (AP)
Foreign Language II	Foreign Language III (H)	Foreign Language IV (AP)	Foreign Language V (AP)
Elective**	Elective**	Elective**	Elective**

* Many top colleges require these courses to incorporate lab lessons.

** Electives are all the college prep courses you take beyond your high school graduation requirement.

36

Now, what do Ivy League schools look for? Of utmost importance, Ivy League schools look for students who have maximized their opportunities and resources. Ivy League schools will also seek applicants with special talents or potential leadership. Therefore, if you stand out in an extracurricular activity, you may get in. Accepted students for Ivy League schools rank in the top 10-15% of their schools. Therefore, they would have taken the most rigorous courses at their high schools. Ivy League Schools and Stanford University recommended courses are below. The information for each subject below is represented as "number of years required" | "number of years recommended":

HIGH SCHOOL ACADEMIC SUBJECTS[2]								
Subjects	English	Fine Arts	Foreign Language	History/ Social Sciences	Math	Science	Science Lab	Social Studies
Brown	4 | 4	2 | 2	3 | 4	2 | 3	3 | 4	3 | 4	2 | -	- | -
Columbia	- | 4	- | -	- | 4	- | 4	- | 4	- | 4	- | -	- | -
Cornell	4 | 4	- | -	- | 3	- | 3	3 | 4	3 | 4	- | -	- | -
Dartmouth	- | 4	- | -	- | 3	- | 3	- | 4	- | 4	- | -	- | -
Harvard	- | 4	- | -	- | 4	- | 3	- | 4	- | 4	- | -	- | -
Princeton	- | 4	- | 1	- | 4	- | 2	- | 4	- | 4	- | 2	- | 2
Stanford	- | 4	- | 1	- | 3	- | 3	- | 4	- | 3	- | 3	- | 3
UPenn	- | 4	- | -	- | 4	- | 3	- | 4	- | 3	- | 3	- | 2
Yale	ND*	ND*	ND*	ND*	ND*	ND*	ND*	ND*

*ND: No data

[2] Common data set of each college

How can you best prepare for Ivy League schools? Take my advice below.

English (4 Years)

Take English classes that will help you to read critically and analytically. These classes cover major novelists, poets, and playwrights. You should take a variety of classes but you should also take English classes that you are passionate about.

Foreign Language (4 Years)

You should be fluent in at least one language other than English. A language skill will broaden your understanding of the world in terms of customs and culture. By the way, stick with one language for four years rather than taking two years of Spanish and two years of French. In recent years, many of my students have taken American Sign Language. This is awesome! You can also volunteer at schools for the hearing impaired and gain community service. This is how you kill two birds with one stone.

History (3 Years)

Take more than an American History class. Take World and European History AP classes too. In today's global village where we are so dependent on one another throughout the world, it helps to take African, Asian, Latin American, or Middle Eastern History. According to Harvard's website, taking three years of history will better prepare you for college than taking courses in economics, comparative government, psychology, sociology or anthropology. But my advice is to take all that you can. You can use the summer breaks to beef up on social science classes.

Math (4 Years)

Try to take algebra and geometry in 7th and 8th grades. One of my students who was accepted to Harvard started with AP calculus AB in 9th grade. This is exceptional but I have seen many students excel in math. Just plan ahead. You should know graphs, exponential and logarithmic function, percentage,  trigonometry, amplitude, period, and phase. Science courses in college require you to know how to estimate orders of magnitude. Social science courses use probability and statistics such as mean, median, mode, and standard deviation so you should take AP statistics as well.

Science (4 Years)

You should take four years of lab science classes. The natural science classes teach human knowledge of our natural world. They stimulate curiosity and our minds through experiments, research, and observations. Basic knowledge in biology, chemistry and physics is essential to understanding scientific discoveries and developments. For top schools take at least biology, chemistry, physics, and two years of advanced study in any of these fields. Anthropology, astronomy, geology, and psychology are not considered substitutes for lab science courses.

How do you know which courses count as core academic courses? When you select your high school course it will say "P" or college prep (CP) course in the course description. On the University of California website, go to www.ucop.edu/doorways. Simply type in your high school (California schools only) and the course name, and it will tell you whether or not it counts as a core academic course or "a-g" as UC calls them. It will also tell you whether the course is an honors or AP class. "a-g" marks required courses that you need to take for UC and if you look next to these subject areas, you'll find little letters in quotations, 'a,' 'b,' 'c,' 'd,' 'e,' 'f,' or 'g.' If you are interested in applying to UC you need to meet the "a-g" course requirement. Check it out.

University of California "a-g" Courses		
Category	**Description**	**Years**
"a" History/Social Science	World history, cultures and geography, U.S. history, civics, American government	2
"b" English		4
"c" Math	Algebra I and II, geometry	3
"d" Laboratory Science	Biology, chemistry, physics	2 (3)
"e" Language other than English	Chinese, Japanese, Korean, Spanish, French, German, Italian, Modern Hebrew, American Sign Language, Greek, Latin	2 (3)
"f" Visual and Performing Arts	Dance, drama, theater, music, or visual arts	1
"g" College Preparatory Electives	(Non-introductory) visual and performing arts, history, social science, English, advanced mathematics, laboratory science language other than English (a third year in the language used for "e" requirement of two years of another language)	1

"I am attending Harvard University studying neurobiology and cognitive science to later attend medical school. Many of my extracurricular activities in high school included a constant theme of helping my community whether it was through volunteer dance and music performances, raising environmental awareness, or scientific research. For the four years in high school, I dedicated myself to working hard academically while balancing my studies with what I love to do, including dance, volunteer work, and simply hanging out with my friends. I hope to work even harder for the next four years and become an even more diverse and well-balanced individual."

Angela Oh, Harvard, Class of 2015
(former Ivy Review student)

2. GPA

For most colleges, the application deadline for Early Decision / Early Action is November 1. The application deadline for University of California schools is November 30. For most colleges, the regular 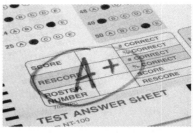 decision application deadline is January 1 or 15. Because the first semester senior grades come out the following January or February, whether you are accepted, rejected or put on the waiting list is decided without your senior first semester grades. In other words, 10th and 11th grades, and the three summers, are the most crucial factors in determining whether or not you get accepted to the college of your choice.

College admissions officers only look at the academic courses listed in your application in order to calculate your GPA. Therefore, you need to calculate your weighted GPA using the academic courses (bible study, cooking, P.E., or health do not count as academic courses) without the senior grades. You need to calculate your GPA based on the rigor of the courses that you have taken. AP, Honors, IB, and college level courses will have a higher score. If you get an A in one of these courses it may count as 5.00.

For current 11th graders, most of your GPA is completed. By the end of your summer, 100% of your GPA will be finished. There is no room for improvement even if you want to work harder at that point.

For current 10th graders, it's just starting. You still have time to improve your grades during summer, 11th grade first and second semesters, and the following summer. This period of time will help determine which college you will attend and spend the next four years of your life.

Your GPA is calculated for two years and three summers, from the summer between 9th and 10th grade to the summer between 11th and 12th grade. Honors, AP, and IB are counted from 10th grade to 12th grade. Therefore, it is important to take as many advanced classes as you can handle in 12th grade too. Although the 12th grade GPA may not factor in for initial admissions, you may get waitlisted, so your senior grades can become an important factor in getting off that list. Therefore, you must still maintain good grades. If you receive a D or F, your admission may be rescinded after you receive the conditional acceptance letter. Remember your high school submits the mid-year report and final report to the colleges after you apply. So you should continue to do well in high school until you get your diploma. According to the National Association for College Admission Counseling's 2009 State of College Admission Report, 21% of the colleges reported that they had rescinded college acceptances in 2008. 65% of acceptances were rescinded because of poor final senior grades.[3] See the rescind numbers for University of California 2010 freshmen. This is serious!

In August of 2010, I received a call from a mother whose daughter had gotten accepted to the University of California, San Diego, which ranked by *U.S. News & World Report* as one of the top 10 public universities in the nation today. Think how happy she was. Think how happy her parents were, proudly saying, "Oh, my daughter got accepted to UCSD!" Unfortunately, she slacked off in her senior year and got a D in AP Spanish, so her acceptance was revoked. Now, she has to go to community college for two years and try to transfer to a four-year college later.

3 http://www.nacacnet.org/PublicationsResources/steps/Articles/Pages/FinishingStrong.aspx

2010 UC Rescind		
Campus	Rescinds	Reasons
Berkeley	17	1. missing documentation
Davis	76	(e.g. transcript not received)
Irvine	150	
Los Angeles	30	
Merced	223	2. academic reasons
Riverside	312	(e.g. D in senior course)
San Diego	38	
Santa Barbara	23	
Santa Cruz	153	

If only she had called me before summer was over. How sad is that? Now, if you do get a D during your senior year, it is not the end of the world. There are ways that you can make up for it in the summer. Colleges strongly urge you to maintain the same level of grades as before during your senior year. However, if for some reason you get a D, immediately contact the admissions office. They want to accept you and work with you, so you can find ways to make up for the poor grade before entering college in the fall. For example, instead of spending that summer before entering college on trips and parties, you might retake the course in community college to make up the D. Now that you get how important it is to maintain strong grades throughout your high school years, let's take a look at how to improve your study skills and test taking strategies.

1) Effective Test Preparation

(A) Be Punctual

At the beginning of class, oftentimes the teacher gives a summary of what she expects to cover that day. Maybe she was behind schedule during the previous class and wasn't able to cover the last chapter. Rushing, she might even blurt out the answers. For standardized tests like the SAT or ACT, what happens if you are one minute late? The test administrator is going to shut that door and you can't go in. You are going to have to wait for the next test, which might be four months down the line, and you may not be able to take the test before the application deadline. So punctuality is very important. Plan to arrive at the test site ten to fifteen minutes early. This way you can get the best seat, get ready for the test, and go to the restroom if needed. Then, no stress!

(B) Sit Where it Counts

For exam purposes, where is the best place to sit? If you do not have a designated seat for the SAT or a final exam—if it's open seating—and the proctor says, "Sit anywhere you want," where is a good place to sit? The front

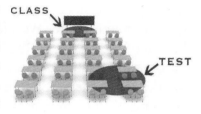

or aisle seat is NOT the best seat. The best place to sit for a test is in the back corner. Why? The proctor will walk back and forth during the test and you'll get distracted if you sit in the front or aisle. You'll think, 'Why is the proctor always walking around me?' Or he might be passing by and brush you, "Oh, excuse me," and break your concentration. But if you are sitting in the back corner against the wall, most likely the proctor will not disturb you. Chances are you will have a nice little bubble, a nice quiet environment in which to focus and concentrate in the back of the room. So, sit in the rear against the wall where proctors have less access and interference. Now, keep in mind, I'm not telling you to sit in the back so you can cheat! It's just the best seat for you to concentrate. Another little tip: in class, try to sit in the front center of the room. Studies have shown that students who sit in the front center tend to get the highest grades and can concentrate more.

(C) See the Big Picture First

Do you remember when you were in 6th or 7th grade, the teacher asked you to do a bunch of things on a piece of paper and at the end it said, "If you had read the instructions first, you would have known that you didn't have had to do any of this." Remember that? Why do you think the teacher made you do that? On the SAT or a final exam, what is the first thing you should do?

The SAT Critical Reading sections are divided into sentence completions, short passages, and long passages. What do the majority of the students do? They jump right into working on question number one. Working question by question towards the end of their Critical Reading passages, they read and solve one question at a time. They look at the clock and they have five minutes left. Then they turn the page and, "Yikes!" There is another critical reading passage. "There's no way I'm going to finish this. I'm dead!" What happened here? They didn't survey the entire section. They didn't know how many questions were in the section. They didn't know how many Critical Reading passages were left or how long the passages were.

This actually happened to one of my students in LA. She thought she was doing well. Usually there are two long critical reading passages in a section. Well, on this particular test, there were three long passages. By the time she got to the third critical reading passage, she did not have sufficient time to finish and she panicked. She ran out of time before she could finish that section. After this critical reading section the next was the math section. She was very good with math but all she could think was how she had messed up the first critical reading section. She could not concentrate. She made silly errors in the math section. What next? She went onto the next section still thinking about the second section she messed up. So throughout the entire test, she was thinking about how badly she did the first critical reading section. And get this, she was a senior taking her last test in December. What should she have done? Number one, she should have looked over the entire section to see how many questions she had. Number two, she should have moved on. It is like playing tennis. You serve, and your ball gets caught in the net and you go, "Darn!" or worse. So you double fault thinking too much. Instead of forgetting about the first lost point and moving on to the next point, if you keep dwelling on that first double fault, it is going to destroy you throughout the game, the first set, and the whole match. So what does your coach tell you to do? "Forget about it. Let it go. Start fresh, brand new." That is what my student needed to do but she didn't.

Let's suppose you are taking a history test and it's a four-part test: the first part is multiple choice, the second part is true or false, the third part is fill in the blank, and the last part is short essay. The essay is worth fifty percent. Which section should you start the test with? THE ESSAY SECTION. You should start with that essay because unless you crank that essay, there is no way you are going to get a passing grade. But many students don't do this. They focus on the first section, the multiple choice section. "Oh, I got these, no problem." Next, true or false, and they go "I got these too. I'm on a roll here." Then, they reach the essay section and run out of time before they can write a good essay. So even if they do all three sections well in the beginning, at best, that's 50%. So they botch that essay, they get a C on the test. That's silly. From time to time, the teachers or professors will throw curves at you like this just to see whether or not you are seeing the big picture first.

47

(D) Get the Sure Points

The other way to look at the big picture is to get sure points. What are the points that count? Do I have to solve test problems in sequence? Absolutely not! You get stuck on number three, thinking, "I've got to do this. No, no, no, I can't move on to number four until I finish number three!" Don't do that. Let it go. You might have a mental block. Let's say the first two problems are on geometry. Then the third problem is on algebra. You might have a mental block because you are thinking geometry. Question number four may be on geometry again. Do number four while you are in the geometry mode. Then come back to number three later.

What's my point? Attack the easy questions first. How are the questions arranged on the SAT? Easy to hardest, in the order of difficulty, except for what? The critical reading sections. Critical reading questions are arranged in the chronological order of the passage: the first questions address the first part of the passage, and the last  questions address the last part of the passage. They also have line cites to indicate where in the passage to look at for the answers. The exceptions are the main idea and tone questions, which could be the first question or the last question for that passage. Now, just because the other SAT questions are arranged in their order of difficulty, this does not mean they go from easy to hard for you. You may be better at geometry than algebra and an algebra problem might be number one. If you don't know how to do it, let it go. Come back only after you are done with the rest of the test.

Do you get extra points for solving difficult problems on the SAT? No. Whether the question is easy or hard, it weighs the same. You do not get bonus points for solving tough questions, so if you get stuck, let it go. Get it? Think about this. Instead of spending thirty seconds and moving on, you spend a minute on the difficult question, and you miss the answer anyways. Not only do you waste time but you also get penalty points for getting the answer wrong. You should have let it go; you should have skipped it. Do you get penalty points on the SAT if you skip? No, you don't get penalty points. So skipping is cool and you could save time and energy for the later problems and sections.

Pick and choose your questions wisely. You are not going to take on a professional boxer, like Mike Tyson. If you get into a ring with him, he's going to cream you. You don't want to die. What's the point? You're wasting your time. You're wasting your strength by taking on a difficult question you can't handle.

(E) Multiple Choice Exams

If you can, try to get an old multiple-choice exam because many teachers recycle them. In the Harvard Library, there are old exams piled up. So students can go in and reference the old exams and study off of them. In your high school, if you have a senior friend who took the same class from the same teacher last year, you could ask him, "Can I borrow your notes? How did you prepare for the final?" That's fair game. That is not cheating. Make sure to ask an 'A' student though.

Now, put yourself in the test maker's shoes. It is not easy making multiple choice questions because the answer choices need to look plausible. Don't get caught in the test maker's traps. You need to verify that each and every word is correct.

In short, answers must be indisputable. Here are some tricks that are used:

- Just one word may make the answer choice wrong. Changing one preposition could change the meaning of the entire sentence.
- The answer choice has a lot of key words that come from the passage so it looks right.
- You see a word related to a word in the question that triggers your instinct. This usually is related to a primary definition of a word.
- There are vague words such as "many" or "things." This often happens for main idea questions.
- There are absolute words such as "never" or "all" in the answer choice. One exception can make that answer wrong so avoid answers with absolute words.

What should you do for short answer questions? Short answer questions are just that. Don't write a dissertation. You'll end up running out of time. Use buzz words. Buzz words are critical for short answers. Teachers are looking for specific types of words. For example, for a question on the Cuban Bay of Pigs Crisis, during the Kennedy administration, you want to use buzz words like "communist," "Cuban dissidents," and "Fidel Castro." These buzz words ought to be in the answer because they are what the teacher is looking for.

2) Term Paper

First, choose a topic you genuinely care about. Second, choose a topic that is marketable. What is marketable? What is hot today? Off the top of your head, list three top current events. Is the War of 1812 a big deal right now? Perhaps not. But

what is relevant? Is the Persian War? Yes, because we have so much conflict with the Persians. So going back to the historical event of the Persian War, the Crusaders may be relevant to where we are today, in terms of Christianity versus Islam. When I drive, I have my radio on the 24-hour news station. I am able to obtain the latest information about statistics that I can use as a conversation piece. If I don't know about current events, I look like an idiot. If I were to say "Oh yeah, we're going through a really bad economy," versus "Yeah, I think the unemployment rate is going to go up to 8.8% by the end of the second quarter," — which sounds better? If I say the latter, people are going to think, "Wow, this guy's smart. He's up-to-date. He even knows the percentage." So read the newspaper daily or watch CNN News or national news such as ABC, NBC, or CBS. Or you can read weekly magazines such as *U.S. News and World Report, Newsweek*, or *Time*. These magazines have the latest relevant news in arts, economy, music, politics, sports, etc. Read and watch the news, so that you can readily use these quotes or statistics in your essays and in your classroom discussions.

Make sure to use various reliable secondary sources. What is a secondary source? It's a document or recording that relates or discusses information originally presented elsewhere, such as a research paper or a newspaper. Is the Internet a reliable secondary source? Sometimes it is, sometimes it is not. So you have to be careful where you get your quotes from. While Wikipedia is a great source to get basic information you cannot use it as a reliable secondary source.

What is a primary source then? It's a source with direct personal knowledge of the events being described. Suppose you are doing research on Vietnam War veterans and you want to know the use of marijuana by U.S. soldiers during that period. If you want to work with a primary source, who do you go to? You would go to the Vietnam vets and say, "Did you use pot? How often? How much?" Chart it up and go to the next vet and say, "Did you use pot? You too? How much? How often?" Then get an average or a percentage of the people who used pot during that period. That is a primary source. In research, when possible, use primary sources. So you will need to type up questionnaires or surveys to directly ask the consumers, teenagers, or your subjects. If you can't, then work from secondary sources that are reliable, such as *The New York Times, The Wall Street Journal, Psychology Today, The Economist, The New England Journal of Medicine,* and other reliable publications or academic journals.

Never set pen to paper until you have a clear idea what you want to talk about. Use words that are precise and meaningful. Clarify your thoughts before you write. Expand on your vocabulary and writing style. Familiarize yourself with proper grammar. Do you have a research project due at the end of the year? How early should you start on it? One month in advance? Two months? Why? Because the more time you have, the more time you have to revise the paper. I have this motto: "In writing, you never finish, you abandon it." What I mean is that you run out of time when you reach the deadline, so you have to abandon it, but there is ALWAYS room for improvement. Writing is an ART. If you have ample time for your college essay or your research project, you can make it sound better and tighten the construction. So spend enough time to prepare so that you don't rush, rush, rush and turn it in prematurely.

Writing Checklist:

- Effective opening sentence
- Smooth narrowing of focus
- Background information provided
- Thesis sentence at the end of the introductory paragraph
- Restatement of thesis in the conclusion paragraph
- Variety of simple, compound, complex, and compound complex sentences
- No sentence fragments
- No run-on or comma splice errors
- Correct use of commas, semicolons, and colons
- No awkward, redundant, or misused words or phrases
- Subject and verb agreement
- Correct use of pronouns
- No dangling or misplaced modifiers
- No shifts in verb tense
- Correct spelling and punctuation

3) How to Retain Vocabulary

(A) Imagery and Mnemonics

How many of you know the word "gregarious?" To me, "gregarious" sounds like gorillas. Imagine a family of gorillas, in a jungle underneath a banana tree. You see a mommy gorilla, baby gorillas, and a daddy gorilla, all chasing one another, playing

around. The gorillas are going, "Woo, woo, woo!" having fun. Right? They are being awfully "sociable." Can you visualize this picture?" Well, gregarious means "SOCIABLE." Now you have "gregarious" associated with an image of these gorillas having fun, being sociable. I kid you not, for the rest of your lives, you will never ever forget the word "gregarious." In fact, many of my former students come to me years later reminiscing about the program and say, "Alex, how you doing? Do you remember that word 'gregarious'? Ha ha," and we get a good kick out of it. Now, you know "gregarious." Before reading this, when you heard the word "gregarious," you would go, "What? What's that? I've heard that before but I'm not sure what that is. Man, it bugs me." If you saw it on the test, you would have been perplexed and said, "Man, I don't know what that is." But now you know. Doesn't that feel good? Someone says "gregarious" and you go "Oh yeah, sociable." Now to retain it, you need to use the word as often as possible. "Jane, you're awfully gregarious today." "Huh, what? Are you cursing at me?" "No, it means sociable. You're awfully friendly today." "Oh, okay." You see? Now, Jane thinks you're smart, "Man, he knows these SAT words." Now you feel better, you feel confident. You are equal to the people who knew the word yesterday.

Here is another word, "taciturn." How do you pronounce it? It is spelled t-a-c-i but let's pretend it is spelled like taxi, t-a-x-i. Imagine a taxi that has to turn a corner quietly so as not to disturb the passengers in the back seat. How? Quietly. Taciturn **TACITURN** means "quiet or silent."

SHHH....

Now you know two SAT words. It's easy and fun because you have an image associated with these words.

Another tactic for retaining vocabulary is to use words that sound similar. For example, "garble" sounds like marble. Imagine a jar full of marbles, all mixed up. Can you guess what "garble" means? Mixed up.

So now, let's review. Now, now, don't turn to the previous page.
What's gregarious?

_____

What's taciturn?

_____

What's garble?

_____

There you go! Great job! We learned three SAT words in a
few minutes. And I kid you not; you will never forget these
words because now you have imagery or a mnemonic device
associated with these words.

(B) Antonyms and Synonyms

Another method of retaining vocabulary is to group words in
antonyms and synonyms. Glue them together. What are some
words that mean, "commonplace"? Trite, hackneyed, banal,
and mundane. These are words that have a similar meaning so
you can use them interchangeably. This is a great way to not
repeat the same word over and over again when you write your
essays as well. The same goes for antonyms. Pairing a word
you know like "modest" with its opposite, "ostentatious," will
help you remember that "ostentatious" means flashy or showy.

(C) Context Clues

You can also guess the meaning of a word through its context.
For example, "John was fired for making an egregious mistake."
What do you think "egregious" means? Do you think that is a
positive or negative word? Negative, since John was fired. "The
eminent scholar brought prestige to her university." "Eminent,"
is it good or bad? It has a positive meaning since the scholar
brought "prestige."

(D) Greek and Latin Roots

A great way to learn vocabulary is by looking at the Greek and Latin roots of the words. For example, the root "am" means love. Words that contain "am" might be related to love: amorous, amicable, and amiable. There are prefixes with negative connotation words: in-, im-, dis-, de-, a-, un-, mal-. Words that start with these prefixes tend to be negative connotation words. Now, I am not saying that every single word that starts with an 'a' is a negative connotation word. "Alex" is obviously not, right? Right!

(E) Harsh and Soft Sounds

You can also use the sound of a word: cantankerous, vexation, and scurrilous. How do they sound? Because of the harsh sounds, they just do not sound positive, do they? Throughout human history we tend to pronounce things that are positive in a nice softer way such as "nice," "soft," and "beautiful."

(F) Make Your Own List

Obviously, you do not do this with all the words you have to learn. Some words just come to you naturally and some words you already know. However, for the words that you constantly having a difficult time memorizing, think of creative ways to retain them. Then the second step is for you to start using these words in your speech and in your writing, so that you retain them, so that you become comfortable with them, and so they become second nature when you use them to talk to people.

What you need to do in terms of improving your vocabulary is to write down all the words that you don't know from now on. It could be a word from a sign on the side of the street while you're in the car with your mom or dad. "What is that word? Serendipity Store. Hmm. Serendipity? That's a really interesting word."

Write it down. While you are reading a newspaper, magazine, textbook, you come across a word, "fastidious." "What the heck is that?" Or maybe you are listening to a political speech or watching TV or a movie and you hear, "pundit." What is that? You write it down. Then, you look up these words as soon as possible. Once you start accumulating a list of words, you will have that much more advantage over students who had let them go. They saw "serendipity" and went, "Hmm, whatever." And then they see it again and go "What is that?" And then hear it on the radio, "serendipity." "Hmm." Four, five, six, seven times and then they finally go, "I'm tired of this. I'm going to look it up." Why do that when you could have done this a month ago, a year ago, when you heard the word for the first time?

You need to learn about 3,000 words to get a perfect score on the Critical Reading section of the SAT. That's a lot of words but chances are throughout your lifetime, in junior high and high school, you have probably learned about 1,000 - 1,500 SAT words already. Remember those vocabulary tests you took in English classes? Let's say we need to learn 2,000 additional words. Now, for an 8th grader, you have the luxury of time: three years, 365 days a year. That's 1,095 days, which means you only have to learn about two words a day. What about juniors? You have to learn 2,000 words in one year. So, 365 days, 2,000 words, what is that approximately? About five or six words a day? You get the picture? It puts a lot more pressure on the juniors. Therefore, it's never too early. I started teaching my two daughters these SAT words when they were four and five years old. Now they're in 9th and 10th grade and they already know many of these words.

You need to know about 3,000 words for the SAT.

"One of the most valuable lessons I learned that has helped me be a successful Yale candidate is to act upon my curiosities and trust my passion for knowledge. As a high school freshman, I began taking courses at my local junior college in anything that seemed interesting: algebra, American Sign Language, Native American anthropology, Art History, and ceramics, to name several of the 12 courses I had taken by graduation. At first, these courses seemed to have little connection to my future endeavors and were merely an interesting and unique opportunity for free learning. While writing my application essays, however, I kept referring to conversations I had with instructors and colleagues from community college. The classes I thought would have no relevance to my future became the rich pools of lessons I could draw upon to create a more cohesive and ambitious plan for college. Furthermore, my passion for learning and interacting with people improved my articulation and matured my professionalism, both necessities at any top-tier university. Colleges do not provide such lessons in soft skills or mannerisms yet such skills are required to hold intellectual conversations. I recognized the value of these achievements in retrospect, yet I would have not come to this realization had I not remained inquisitive or audacious. To those seeking a fruitful higher education: Be driven by the passions and curiosities you have, whatever those may be, and even if they seem irrelevant or contradictory. If you trust yourself and the words of your mentors, your passions will drive you to your destination."

Christine Jun, Yale, Class of 2012
(former Ivy Review student)

3. AP / IB / HONORS / COLLEGE LEVEL COURSES

Make sure you understand that you don't have to take AP level for all your courses. You should take as many as YOU can handle. It is better to take two AP classes and get all As than to take four AP classes and get two Cs. You can take community college or four-year college courses during the summer to make up for one or two fewer AP classes. You can take two AP courses in high school and then take two college level courses at a community college. This way it becomes the equivalent of taking four AP classes at your high school. Many junior and senior students tell me that they are taking five AP classes next year. When I ask them why, their answer is, "Because that's what all my friends are doing." Be cautious. If you get too stressed and cannot keep up and receive Cs, then your GPA will go down big time. You don't want that. Therefore, it is prudent to take only as many AP classes as you can handle. However, when you sign up for classes, it is always better to sign up for AP, and then switch to a regular class if it becomes too hard to handle. It is easy to go to your counselor and say that you want to change to a regular class. Usually, you can't take a regular class and then try to move up to AP class. Counselors do not let you go up to AP classes because of the summer reading materials required for AP classes. Also by the time you want to sign up for AP, the class may be full.

During summertime you should try to take at least one class at a community college or university. If you take a summer class at high school it may not be as productive. Most high schools don't offer AP or Honors classes during summer. So, if you take summer school at high school, an A will only count as 4.0. Whereas, if you take a college level course and you get an A, it may count as $4.0 + 1.0 = 5.0$ grade because it's a college level course. Let's say your weighted GPA right now is 4.3. If you take high school summer school, your GPA is going to go down even if you get an A because it will count as 4.0. Get it? But if you take a college level course and you get an A, your GPA is going to go up. So take community college or university courses rather than courses at your high school during the summer.

In addition to community colleges and four-year colleges, there are a few websites where you can go to take online AP or college level classes. Brown, Cornell, Harvard, Stanford, and Brigham Young University are a few colleges that offer online courses. You can take the online courses at the convenience of your home. Michael Oher, NFL American football offensive tackle, who is also the inspiration for the movie, *The Blind Side*, took advantage of the BYU online courses to meet the NCAA GPA requirements. He replaced Fs with improved grades from BYU courses. This is how you bring up your weighted GPA and impress the admissions officers. And yes, you can take them as a high school student.

Brown University Online Pre-College Courses:
> *http://onlinecourselearning.com/brown/#*

Cornell University School of Continuing Education and Summer Sessions Online Courses:
> *http://www.sce.cornell.edu/ss/courses/courses. php?action=roster&f=DL_STATUS&v=1*

Harvard University Extension School Distance Education:
http://www.extension.harvard.edu/distance-education

Brigham Young University Independent Study:
> *http://is.byu.edu/is/site/*

Sometimes your high school counselor may discourage you from taking community college courses, university courses, and online courses. They may also say that the A you get from that community college Psychology course may not count towards your high school GPA. First, high schools prefer their students to take courses from within the high school rather than go to other institutions to take these courses. Second, there is a difference between high school graduation requirements and college entrance evaluations. Are there any specific colleges or community colleges I should go to? Each school will be different in terms of admissions procedures, age requirements, start dates, course length and units etc. You will need to check with each school individually. The bottom line is you need to take college level courses rather than personal enhancement courses such as how to photoshop. In choosing the course, you want to check out the professors who teach the courses beforehand. Go to www.ratemyprofessors.com, www.myedu.com, and www.courserank.com. At these websites, you can get information about the professors and courses. The students rate the professors and write reviews, so you know which teachers to avoid. If he is a lousy teacher, you probably don't want to take his course.

> *Ratemyprofessors.com*
> *Myedu.com*
> *Courserank.com*

While the college, community college and online courses may not be factored into your high school GPA, college admissions officers will take those courses into account when they evaluate your application. So, when you apply to college, you need to send the official transcripts from all the institutions that you took courses from rather than only your high school transcript. In evaluating the courses you took at colleges, community colleges, and online, the admissions officers at the colleges you apply to will compare the course to what they offer at their own schools. If the level and curriculum is comparable to a course they offer, they will accept it as a college level course and include it in your evaluation. Make sure to take the course from an accredited institution.

4. AP EXAMS

As you may know, you can take the AP exams only once a year in May. Therefore, it is better to take the exams throughout 9th, 10th, and 11th grades. There is no place in the application to write AP scores taken in 12th grade. If you get three points out of five on the AP exam, you will get credit at UC. However, for Stanford and Ivy League schools you need to get four or five to get credit for the AP courses. That's why you need to take AP exams in your freshman, sophomore or junior years. However, Harvard does not offer any credits for AP exams. Still, it looks good to have 5's on the AP exams, right?

AP score reports are sent to the colleges you request on the registration sheet in July. If you do not receive a score report by September 1, you should contact AP Services. The AP score reports are cumulative and include all the AP exam scores you have taken unless you request that the AP score be withheld or canceled. If you want to send your AP scores to additional colleges you can request those by phone, mail, or fax at a fee of $15 per college. The additional reports usually take about one week and you can also request a rush report, which will be sent in two working days.

The AP exams are given during two weeks in May at 8 am, 12 pm, and 2 pm. You can only take the exams on the dates and in the locations designated by the College Board. If you would like to take exams that are scheduled for the same time, make sure to schedule late-testing exams.

The College Board offers AP exams for the following courses:

- Art History
- Biology
- Calculus AB
- Calculus BC
- Chemistry
- Chinese Language and Culture
- Comparative Government and Politics
- Computer Science A
- English Language and Composition
- English Literature and Composition
- Environmental Science
- European History
- French Language and Culture
- German Language and Culture
- Human Geography
- Italian Language and Culture
- Japanese Language and Culture
- Latin: Vergil
- Macroeconomics
- Microeconomics
- Music Theory
- Physics B
- Physics C: Mechanics
- Psychology
- Spanish Language
- Spanish Literature
- Statistics
- Studio Art
- United States Government and Politics
- United States History
- World History

What should you do if you have a low AP score that you do not want to be sent to the colleges you are applying to? First, you can have the score canceled. When you cancel the score, it will be permanently deleted from your records. You can cancel an AP score at any time but if you don't want it to be on the current year's score report, you have to make the cancellation request to AP Services by mail or fax by June 15. Second, you can request that an AP score be withheld from a college. To do this, you should send the request by mail or fax to AP Services by June 15 with a fee of a $10 per score, per college. You can later ask AP Services to release that score if you want. One point to remember, a withheld score is NOT deleted from your records and will be sent to you and your high school.

To contact the College Board regarding AP exams:

AP Services

P.O. Box 6671

Princeton, New Jersey 08541-6671

Phone: 888-225-5427 (toll-free in the United States and Canada
        609-771-7300

Email: apexams@info.collegeboard.org

"In an application pool that becomes more competitive each year, how do you make yourself stand out? How does an admissions office decide to accept you over another student with similar academic and extracurricular achievements? A strong "personal appeal" to the school is critical. Personal appeal is how you portray yourself to the school, and how others (interviewers and teachers) perceive you. It develops from the personal essay, recommendations, and interviews. You should be able to explain your uniqueness, how you can link yourself to the school and contribute to its environment, and how the school can help you achieve your goals. "Personal appeal" should ultimately answer two questions for the admissions office: 1) How much do you want to attend this school?; and 2) How much does the school want you to attend? I fortunately had personal connections (summer programs, campus visits, relatives, or professors) that I used in my personal essays or recommendations (e.g. I had teachers who attended Columbia and Harvard write recommendations for those schools). Having excellent "personal appeal" helped me most in gaining entrance to every school to which I had applied" (Brown, Columbia, Duke, Emory, GA Tech, Harvard, Johns Hopkins, MIT, and Yale).

Trevor Thompson, Harvard, Class of 2011

5. SAT REASONING TEST

In order to do well on the SAT, you need some basic math skills, vocabulary, grammar, and critical thinking skills. You also need to be a good test taker. Remember! The SAT is not like the tests you take in school; it has a different structure, and success on it requires different types of test-taking skills. Studying is like playing sports. Think of this book as your coach. It could give you all the techniques for improving your scores, but if you don't practice, you will not improve. It's the same thing with studying. It may be awkward in the beginning. It could be stuff that you have never learned before. You will go, "Huh?" "What?" "No way?" "Way!" It works. Remember to practice each skill and technique to make it work for you.

1) Understanding the Format of the SAT

How long is the test? Long! There are three critical reading sections, three math sections, three writing sections, and one experimental section: ten sections for three hours and forty-five minutes. The experimental section, which is 25 minutes, is not scored and it could be a critical reading, math, or writing section.

Section	#	Timing	Question Types	Scoring
Critical Reading	3	Two 25-minute sections & One 20-minute section	Critical Reading Short Reading Passages Sentence Completions	200-800
Math	3	Two 25-minute sections & One 20-minute section	Regular Math Grid-Ins	200-800
Writing	3	One 25-minute section & One 10-minute section One 25-minute essay	Grammar, usage, and word choice Written Essay	200-800
Experimental	1	One 25-minute section	Critical Reading, Math, or Writing	N/A
Total	10	3 hours 45 minutes		600-2400

What do you need to get in order to get into top universities? About 700 across or 2,100 in total. For Ivy League schools, MIT, Stanford, or Cal Tech you need to get at least 760, 760, and 760. So for example, if you receive 800 in math, but you got 700 in writing and 800 in critical reading, even though the combined score is 2300 you may need to retake the test because your writing score is 700. In other words, they do look at the split scores not merely the total score. Remember this. There is always an exception. Therefore, it is neither a guarantee nor an automatic rejection if you do not get these scores but just to be on the safe side, this is the comfort zone you want to be in.

Freshmen SAT Scores (Mid 50%) [4]			
Scores are represented as low score | average score | high score			
Colleges	SAT Verbal	SAT Math	SAT Combined
Brown	660 | 710 | 760	670 | 720 | 770	1,985 | 2,135 | 2,285
Columbia	680 | 725 | 770	690 | 735 | 780	2,045 | 2,180 | 2,315
Cornell	630 | 680 | 730	670 | 720 | 770	1,940 | 2,090 | 2,240
Dartmouth	670 | 720 | 770	680 | 730 | 780	2,015 | 2,165 | 2,315
Harvard	690 | 745 | 800	700 | 745 | 790	2,075 | 2,225 | 2,375
Princeton	690 | 740 | 790	710 | 750 | 790	2,090 | 2,225 | 2,360
Stanford	670 | 715 | 760	690 | 740 | 790	2,030 | 2,172 | 2,315
UPenn	660 | 705 | 750	690 | 735 | 780	2,015 | 2,150 | 2,285
Yale	700 | 750 | 800	700 | 740 | 780	2,090 | 2,225 | 2,360

[4] Source: Common Application

2) Scoring

Do you know what you get if you sign your name and go to sleep for three hours and forty-five minutes? $200 + 200 + 200 = 600$ points across all three sections. That's right; you can't get a zero on the SAT. So relax. The SAT scoring works as follows:
- You get 1 point for each correct answer.
- You lose a fraction of a point for each wrong answer.
- You neither lose nor gain points for an answer left blank.

3) Order of Difficulty

With the exception of Critical Reading questions, all questions are arranged in the order of difficulty. That is, the questions get harder as you move along. You can use this bit of knowledge to your advantage if you remember the following: (A) Answer all easy questions first. (B) Save the hard questions for later. If you find an easy answer to a hard question, beware. Double and triple check because sometimes the obviously easy answer will have one word that makes it wrong. Each and every word in the answer choice must be correct. The SAT is about choosing the BEST answer not a good answer.

4) Answering the Questions

It is important to remember that you do not have to answer the questions in order. You can skip around within each section. You should attack the questions you find easiest first and never spend more than 30 seconds on any one question. Just be careful when marking your answers on the answer bubble sheet. Remember these two rules that go together:

(A) When you encounter a tough question, circle or check it and move on.
(B) Return to the difficult questions only after you have completed all the easy questions.

5) Guessing

You want to score high on the SAT? Learn how to make an educated guess. A good guessing strategy is one of the most important skills to develop in order to maximize your points on the SAT. There are two types of guessing: random and educated. There are five multiple-choice answers: A, B, C, D, E. If you don't have the foggiest idea and cannot get rid of any of the five answer choices, skip it. But if you can eliminate two or even one answer choice, always guess, because the odds are in your favor that you will get the correct answer. Go with your gut feeling, the shortest answer, whatever it is that makes sense to you.

Ivy Review's Guessing Strategy

Skip = If I can't eliminate any of the five answers

Go with Instinct = If I can eliminate one out of five answers

Rank 1, 2, 3 = If I can eliminate two out of five answers

Always Guess = If I can eliminate three out of five answers

Another strategy you need to consider is the penalty for missed questions. You do not want to answer too many questions blindly. For example, in section 2, let's say there are 35 writing questions. You answer every single one of them. You get 15 right, you miss 20. You get a quarter point taken off for each one you missed. So you divide the number of incorrect answers by four ($20 \div 4 = 5$) or minus five points. So you subtract five from fifteen ($15 - 5 = 10$), your raw score for that section is 10 points. Do you know what that means? Had you sat there for twenty-five minutes and answered only 11 questions correctly and skipped 24 questions, you would have gotten a higher score. Not to mention, you would have been less tired at the end of sections 9 and 10 because you shortened the test. Now, you have time to read the questions once, twice, and even three times. So that's what I want you to do. But wait. What if you only answer 11 questions and you get some of those wrong? Then you would fall below your target score of 11. So you need to add a buffer zone. In other words, instead of answering all 35 questions, just answer 21 questions. Yes, just answer 21 questions. You are going to still skip 14 questions, especially the ones that are hard. So you are going to pick and choose the ones that you are going to answer. If you miss some of the 21 questions, let's say six or seven, you are still over your target score that you want to reach. But—here is a big BUT—as a rule of thumb, if you want to get a score of 700 or higher in all three sections or 2100 total, you should NOT skip any questions. But if your target is below 700, you actually can get a higher score by answering a fewer number of questions.

6) SAT Converted Scores

How many critical reading questions are there on the SAT? There are a total of sixty-seven critical reading questions. How many questions can you skip and still get 800? You can skip two, sometimes three, questions and still get a perfect 800 score. In order for you to get 600 on the SAT I Critical Reading, what is the raw score that you need to get? 600 equals approximately a raw score of 42. That means you can skip how many questions and still get 600? $67 - 42 = 25$. You could skip 25 and still get 600, which is still a respectable score and 100 points over the national average.

How many math questions are on the SAT? Fifty-four. You can't miss any in order to get a perfect score. But if you miss two, you would probably get 780 or 760. How about writing? How many writing questions are there on the SAT? Forty-nine. That's it. It seems like there are a ton of these questions but there are only 49 questions. If you miss or skip one of the grammar or paragraph revision questions, your score may be 580 out of 600. The essay in the first section counts for 200 points.

Let's say you got a 500 on the critical reading section. 500 translates into how many raw score points? It depends on the test but approximately 25. For the next practice test, let's say you want to improve fifty points so you get 550. In order to get a 550 on critical reading, how many more questions do you have to get right? About 33. So you need to get essentially eight more questions right next time you take a practice test in order to improve fifty points.

7) When is the Best Time to Take the SAT?

You can take the SAT in October, November, December, January, March, May or June. Colleges have different policies regarding SAT scores. Stanford and Harvard accept the "superscores" or the highest scores for each section even from multiple test dates. UC only accepts the test scores from a single sitting. If you know the evaluation method of each college you want to apply to beforehand, it would help you get ready for the SAT. If the school selects the highest scores, you can focus on math during the January SAT and focus on reading during the May test.

So, when is the best time to take the SAT? Contrary to popular belief, there is no "easy" test month. There is no guarantee you will improve 200 points after studying for two months. The best time to take the SAT depends on two things: what your target score is and how ready you are to take the SAT. One thing for sure is that you do not have to wait until you are in 11th or 12th grade to take the SAT. If Ashley starts to prepare for the test early and is completely ready in 9th grade—let's say she averages a 2200 to 2300—I would recommend that she take the test now. Get it over with! There is no regulation against taking the test in 9th grade. Therefore, if you are ready, take it now, in your freshman, sophomore or junior year. Don't wait until you are a senior. Start the preparation early. Prepare to take the test for the first time in December and the second time in January of your 10th grade, or at least 11th grade. When you are preparing to take the SAT, skip that ski trip. Stay home and study. Get it over with in January. Then, you can relax and enjoy snowboarding during your spring break. Otherwise, you have to study for the SAT again and again. You will have to study for the SAT during the summer and take it in October of your 12th grade. Try not to do this.

The last SAT you can take for college admissions is December of your senior year. But try to avoid taking the test in December; this is the time when you are finalizing your college applications. In addition, during your senior year, you're going to have many AP classes and you have little time to prepare for the SAT. So you want to try and finish the SAT and SAT IIs by the end of your junior year. And to do so, you need to prep for it in the 8th, 9th and 10th grades.

Therefore, I recommend that you take the real SAT when you are ready, when you are at your peak. However, it is more impressive for a freshman to get a 2400 on the SAT than for a senior. When you submit your applications, admissions officers recognize this and will go, "Wow! Ashley took the SAT I in her freshman year and got a 2400. Let her in." So start early and finish early!

Admissions officers will be more impressed with a perfect score from a freshman than a junior.

8) Don't Despair About Your First SAT Test Results

The national average across the three test sections is approximately 500, 500, 500, for juniors and seniors who take the SAT. So if you are a freshman or sophomore and get around 500 for each section, you are doing really well. Now, is that good enough? It depends on which college you want to go to.

I expect you to improve your SAT scores.
It's doable because for math, one question is worth as much as 10 points. So, if you get one or two more questions correct, your score will go up. In addition, because you didn't know about the penalty points, you answered all the questions and got penalized for having wrong answers. So once you know how to take the test, your scores will go up eventually. As I tell my thousands of students, many of my top students started about the same or even lower than the national average score, but they gradually went up. However, it takes hard work. It doesn't happen automatically. You have to put in the EFFORT and TIME.

So next time you take an SAT practice test, and you want to improve a total of 150 points, or 50 per section, it is a realistic goal. You just need to make incremental targets. No one was born with a 2400 score. Wherever you started, you have to learn how to walk first. Then, you learn how to jog. And then you learn how to sprint. One step at a time. One of my students improved 510 points after four lectures. What did she do? Develop a super brain overnight? No. She worked her tail off and also applied these strategies when taking the test.

9) How to Prepare for Critical Reading

Not everyone loves to read. For the Critical Reading section of the SAT, you need to read analytically. You have to obtain vital information; identify main ideas and sub ideas; get the author's intent; and so on. Keep in mind that the SAT does not test you on the subject matter. Rather, they want to know if you understand the big picture: What is the primary purpose? Why is the author thinking this way? Why does the author use one word over the other? The passages for the critical reading sections come from literature, natural science, social science, arts, and humanities. There are six types of questions for the critical reading and once you identify the question type and apply the strategies for it, you will be able to critically analyze the passage and the answer choices and narrow down your answer choices.

10) How to Prepare For Writing

What's in the SAT writing section? First, there is a 25-minute essay. Then, there are two sections, one that is 25 minutes and one that is 10 minutes which cover the following: sentence improvement, grammatical error identification, and paragraph revisions. Grammatical error identification is straight, simple grammar. The SAT does not test all areas of grammar. There are about twenty grammar rules that you need to know and identify. To name a few: sentence-verb agreement, verb tense, idioms, diction, parallelism, modifiers, etc. For sentence improvement, you have to look at the style, expression, structure, and standard usage. So you will look for awkwardness, wordiness, passive versus active voice, run-on sentences, sentence fragments, etc. Paragraph revision is all about combining sentences, creating a different order of the sentences, or deleting sentences, so essentially you become an editor for that section. There are about fifteen questions that come out again and again. You just need to know how to answer these questions based on the passage. So once you know the name of the game it's not that bad. It's not like you are fighting blind, swinging as hard as you can with your eyes closed and hopefully landing a blow on your opponent. You conserve your energy, strategically walking around jabbing and looking for an empty spot to hit an upper cut.

11) How to Prepare For Math

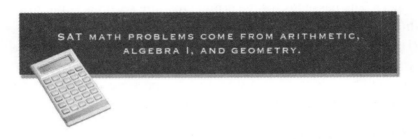

SAT MATH PROBLEMS COME FROM ARITHMETIC, ALGEBRA I, AND GEOMETRY.

Now, what about math? SAT covers basic arithmetic, algebra (I and II) and geometry. That's it. You don't need trigonometry, calculus, or math analysis; no sine or cosine stuff. So if you have taken Algebra and Geometry, you have all the necessary knowledge to obtain a perfect score on the math section. Why? Because you took it in school already, you're supposed to understand these theorems and formulas, how to set up problems, etc. Then, why aren't you getting an 800? One reason might be you took Algebra so far back that you forgot. A second theory might be your math teacher sucked so you really didn't learn much. Or maybe you were absent that critical time when the teacher was teaching the Pythagorean Theorem because you had a dentist appointment. Or maybe you caught a cold or flu and you missed some class. So what? Now relearn it. In math, you either know it or you don't. Remember you are equipped with all the math knowledge you need to ace the math section. Just practice, practice, practice.

12) How to Prepare for the Essay

The SAT essay gives you a short passage to give you background information and put you in the right mindset for the question. Then you get a question that asks you whether you agree or disagree. Your task is to choose a side and support your argument with examples from your readings, studies, experience, and observations.

(A) Analyze the Question and Interpret it into Your Own Words

What does that mean? You need to know what the test maker is asking. For example, "Every cloud has a silver lining." Suppose you see this as your essay question. What does that mean to you? No idea? You'd be in trouble if that was the SAT essay prompt. It means that every bad part has some goodness to it. Let's take 9/11 for example. Many people were murdered, it was a tragic event; innocent lives were lost. But what good came out of that? Better airline security perhaps? Scrutinizing terrorists through intelligence? We became a more alert society. Let's say something tragic happened in your life. For example, your dog died. What good came out of that? Maybe because of that you understand and appreciate pets even more. So something good came out of this tragedy. Interpret the essay question in your own words.

Fortunately, most of the essay questions can be grouped together. Some of the repeated topics are creativity, ethics, individuality, loyalty, success, technological progress, etc. Your examples to support your essay should come from literature, history, and current events. You also need to keep up with the world. One of the March 2011 SAT essay questions asked about reality shows. If you have no idea what a reality show is you would be in trouble.

(B) Narrow the Question Down

The essay questions are going to be broad, so you need to narrow them down. How do you do this? Come up with an argument that addresses the topic in a specific context. The best way to do this is to start by choosing an example. For an essay question, "History repeats itself," you might choose to write about how the French Revolution deposed one dictator only to replace him with another dictator who later needed to be deposed. You could also talk about how discrimination is a constant in all cultures, in all time periods. To disagree with this topic you could point out how a particular invention, such as the computer, has forever altered some aspect of our society.

(C) Write Your Outline

Should I make an outline for an essay? Absolutely! It will give you an idea about what you are going to talk about before you start writing. Jot down your general argument and note the point you wish to make in each paragraph.

(a) Introduction

Power is a corrupting force, which causes humans to repeat the mistakes of their predecessors.

(b) How this idea is illustrated by the events of the French Revolution.

(c) How this idea is illustrated by the book Animal Farm.

(d) (Optional) How children repeat many of the mistakes their parents made with them.

(e) Conclusion

As soon as the proctor says, "You may start the test," 95% of the students are going to start writing immediately after they read the question. I guarantee you that their organization and structure will be flawed. You, on the other hand, will sit there for two minutes, analyze the question and make a decent outline before you actually start drafting the paper. You hear the other students start writing, pencil scratching against paper and you see that they are almost at the end of their first paragraph. On the other hand, you haven't gotten anything on your piece of paper. Don't panic, it's ok. You might get a little nervous but you've got everything under control. Why? Because you are going to create a better essay with an outline.

(D) Start Your Essay with an Attention Grabber

An introduction should begin with an interesting yet broad opening sentence. The idea is to grab the reader's attention. The following are different types of effective beginnings:

(a) Short Generalization

"It is a miracle that New York works at all."

(b) Startling Claim

"It is possible to stop most drug addiction in the United States within a very short time."

(c) Rhetorical Question

"How is it possible to adequately punish a murderer? What solution does murdering the murderer bring?"

(d) Statistical Data

Suppose I say, "These days a lot of high school boys smoke cigarettes in high school." What a general and vague statement! Compare that to, "According to the September 2009 issue of *The New England Journal of Medicine*, approximately 73.5% of the male population in high school has experimented with some form of tobacco smoking." Big difference. You've got the reference, the journal. You've got statistics. It grabs the reader's attention.

(E) Have a Clear Thesis Statement in Your Introduction

Make sure your introduction includes the thesis statement that clearly states your central argument and why you feel this way. The thesis is the backbone of your entire essay. In one sentence, it expresses the main argument that the essay will make. To alert your reader to your main point as soon as possible, the thesis should be articulated clearly in the introduction. Customarily, it is placed at the very end of the introductory paragraph.

As you write your thesis statement, keep in mind that the sentence should make an argument and should, therefore, be disputable. But don't add the word "sometimes" in the thesis. Since it is an argument we already know that it is not a 100% true fact. You are expressing your opinion. In addition, your thesis needs to respond to the essay prompt and address each of its component parts. Answer the question! You wouldn't believe how many students start writing and digress from the prompt. Therefore, before writing the thesis, you need to carefully read the assigned topic. As you read, try to break the topic down into its component parts. Most topics deal with a particular subject, about which they then make an assertion, with which you need to agree or disagree. Your thesis should thus address the subject, make an assertion about it, and then explain WHY you feel that way. The "WHY" is the key to getting 12 out of 12 on the SAT essay.

(F) Make Sure Every Paragraph Has a Clear and Distinct Point

What do you want to start the body paragraphs with? The TOPIC SENTENCE. The topic sentence states the main idea of that paragraph. How many ideas should there be in each paragraph? Only one idea. So if you start talking about something that is not included in that topic sentence, what do you need to do? Start a new paragraph.

(G) Close Your Essay with a Powerful Statement

The conclusion must communicate to the reader that what you have written is of lasting significance and relevance. How do I do that? A bunch of exclamation points? No. Your concluding paragraph is your last chance to persuade the reader. Therefore, you should avoid ending on a personal note such as "I think..." or "In my opinion..." These are as ineffective at the end as they are in the beginning of an essay. In addition, the concluding paragraph is not the place to bring in any new ideas, new evidence, or added appeals. Force yourself not to do this. Remind your readers only of your most important points; refresh their memories at the end.

The final word is do not present an ambivalent opinion. In other words, do NOT leave your readers in doubt as to where you stand. Do NOT end your essay with a question or an indecisive statement that asks readers to investigate the problem further or to decide for themselves. They are reading your essay to find the answers to their questions not just to get more questions. Remember you are the master of your essay.

(H) Do Not Use Vague Words such as *Thing* or *Stuff*, or Ambiguous Pronouns such as *This* or *That*

I noticed that a lot of students use "thing." For example, after SAT class, you get into mom or dad's car, and the first thing they ask is, "So how was class today?" "Fine." "What did you learn?" "Things." "Stuff." "I don't know." Mom's going, "You did what? I'm spending all this time and money for your education and you're learning STUFF?" You could generalize by saying things and stuff. However, you SHOULD narrow it down to details. For example, you could say, "I learned about critical reading strategies and how to attack the SAT essay with four paragraphs."

What is the point here? When you write an essay, don't write words such as, *things, stuff, like* etc. I notice that many students use "like." "You know *like* I was over there *like*, seven times *like*." Repeatedly. It becomes *like* habit forming, *like*, you know? When I interviewed applicants for Harvard, students would say, "You know, like, throughout my high school like, I like to do this, and you know, like…" and I go, "Huh? What are you talking about?" Avoid vague words and find a substitute that will pinpoint what you actually want to talk about.

(I) Use No More Words than Necessary to Express What You Want to Say

In writing, succinct is the best form. The shorter, the better. Be concise. When you see yourself repeating yourself, that's when you get into trouble. Redundancy is your enemy. Make each sentence count.

(J) Common Essay Pitfalls to Avoid

(a) Don't be vague or wishy-washy

All this shows is that you are not sure what you're talking about. Come up with one solid opinion, stick to it, and end with it.

(b) Don't use street jargon, colloquialisms, or rhetoric

What's a colloquialism? It's everyday conversation language. For example, I might say, "Wow, Sarah, those sunglasses you have on are pretty cool." I don't mean temperature cool, do I? I mean they're nice sunglasses. That is colloquial. We don't want to use that in the formal writing. So you don't "hang out with your friends," you "socialized." You don't "ace the test," you "passed the test." You don't "get it," you "understand." Get it?

Another point you should remember for academic essays is "NO CONTRACTIONS." "Don't," "It's," "You're," etc., don't belong in formal writing. Always write it out; "Do not," "It is," and "You are." I know it sounds awkward because we don't usually talk like this, but you have to keep in mind the SAT essay is there to assess your formal academic writing skills. Hey! What about this book? It's got all these contractions! Hey! This is not an SAT essay!

(c) Don't overwrite or underwrite

What is overwriting? It means that you spend time dwelling on one specific issue and consequently, you miss the boat. Sometimes when students use a literary example, they end up writing a book report. Only add the relevant information about your example. On the other hand, don't be too lazy or abruptly end by just mentioning an idea without adding details, and moving on to the next topic either. This leaves the reader wondering why you brought up the idea and how it ties into your thesis.

(K) Revise! Revise! Revise!

There is no end to writing. Every time you read your essay, there will be something you could change to make it better. Also, you need to meticulously proofread for grammatical errors, spelling, punctuation, etc. Keep in mind all the writing areas that are tested on the multiple-choice section of the SAT writing section. So save yourself ample time to proofread, about five minutes at the end.

13) Contact Information

If you want to contact the College Board about the SAT:

Web: http://www.collegeboard.com/student/testing/sat/about.html

Telephone: Domestic: (866) 756-7346 International: (212) 713-7789

Mail: College Board SAT Program P.O. Box 025505, Miami, FL 33102

6. SAT SUBJECT TESTS

Most top private colleges require at least two to three SAT subject tests. For Stanford, the SAT subject tests are not required but they do highly recommend applicants to submit them. UC's policy for SAT subject tests changed from 2012. Students applying to UC from 2012 will no longer have to take SAT subject tests unless you are applying to a specific major. Harvard requires two SAT Subject Tests and wants you to show breadth in academic interest by taking tests in different subject matters. You should not submit two subject tests in math nor should you submit a subject test in your first language if your first language is not English. Additional subject tests are encouraged as evidence of the breadth and depth of your academic accomplishments. What does this mean? If you are a student whose first language is Chinese and are interested in engineering, you could submit Math IIC, Spanish, and Physics.

You can take the SAT subject tests in October, November, December, January, May, and June. In March, you cannot take SAT subject tests. The subjects offered each month differ from month to month, so you need to plan ahead. You need to select the subject tests you will take when registering. You may change which subject tests you take on the actual test day except for the listening test. You may take up to three SAT Subject Tests on a single test date. The SAT language tests with listening such as Chinese, Japanese, and Korean are only offered in November so be careful not to miss the registration deadline since you can only take them once a year. The language with listening tests are in the first hour of testing so you can take only one listening test per year. Also, the language with listening tests are not offered to walk-in students.

Which SAT subject tests should you take? If you plan to go to medical school, take biology, chemistry or physics, especially if you plan to apply to a private school. It is better to take subject tests related to your prospective major. For example, if you want to major in liberal arts, take the literature, U.S. history, world history or foreign language tests. The best time to take the SAT subject tests is in May when you take the AP exams. Then, if you need to retake them, you can take them once more in June and be done with them. If you are taking AP Chemistry now, take the SAT chemistry test in May or June even if you are in 10th grade. This way the material is fresh in your mind. You do not have to prepare for the tests separately. Just focus on the material from school. Do not spend a lot of money preparing for SAT subject tests.

Month	Subject Tests		
October	U.S. History	Physics	Mathematics Level 2
	Literature	French	Mathematics Level 1
	Chemistry	Spanish	Biology E/M
November	U.S. History	Chinese with Listening	Spanish with Listening
	Literature	French with Listening	Korean with Listening
	Chemistry	German with Listening	Mathematics Level 2
	Physics	Japanese with Listening	Mathematics Level 1
			Biology E/M
December	U.S. History	Physics	Spanish
	World History	Latin	Mathematics Level 2
	Literature	French	Mathematics Level 1
	Chemistry	Italian	Biology E/M
January	U.S. History	Physics	Mathematics Level 2
	Literature	French	Mathematics Level 1
	Chemistry	Spanish	Biology E/M
March	No subject tests		
May	U.S. History	Spanish	Mathematics Level 2
	Literature	Physics	Mathematics Level 1
	Chemistry	French	Biology E/M
June	U.S. History	Latin	Spanish
	World History	Modern Hebrew	Mathematics Level 2
	Literature	French	Mathematics Level 1
	Chemistry	German	Biology E/M
	Physics		

7. WRITE AN AWESOME COLLEGE ESSAY

Most of the seniors who apply to college start writing their essays the day after Thanksgiving. They procrastinate! They say, "I'm too busy with school work right now. I have to study for the SAT. I'll start working on my college essay later." When is later? When later comes, you say, "Oh, I'm too tired. I'll start next week." And another week goes by. The next thing you know, it's Christmas. Now, you only have one week to finish the essay and submit it by the January 1 deadline. Believe me, I don't care how good of a writer you are, you cannot come up with an awesome college essay in one week. You need sufficient time to work on it. So start preparing for the essays early on.

The college essay has to be a special story about yourself. It is better to talk about any hardships you have faced. Do not be ashamed of your hardships. We can break down hardships into three categories: physical hardships, family hardships, and financial hardships.

1) Hardships

(A) Physical Hardships

The first hardship is physical hardship. For example, "I got injured when I was in high school so I missed classes to go to the hospital. Even though I tried hard to catch up in my studies I was able to only get a B- in my AP U.S. history class." You could be sight impaired, or hearing impaired. This is nothing to be ashamed about. It is to your advantage to talk about any disease or sickness that you have rather than trying to hide it. But don't make it up!

(B) Family Hardships

The second hardship is family hardship. For example, your parents got divorced. Now, in the case of your parents' divorce, it needs to have taken place when you are in high school. If your parents' divorce occurred when you were in elementary school, it does not become a hardship you can describe. Other incidents would be something in the nature of, "My mother had a major car accident," or "My father became ill." You can mention your grandparents' illnesses if they live with you. But if your grandmother who lives in another state or country and you see once a year passes away, that wouldn't be considered a hardship. Some people try to make the death of a pet into a hardship, but unless it's a really compelling story, it usually does not work. Family hardships deal with any immediate members of your family. Your brother or sister did drugs, joined a gang, dropped out of school, became ill so you had to take care of him or her. Your brother has Down syndrome and you have to take care of him because both of your parents work. These are all examples of family hardships.

(C) Financial Hardships

The third is a financial hardship. Examples of financial hardships are: your dad is unemployed, the family business is hit by the bad economy, or your father filed for bankruptcy. Maybe your dad lives in another country, and you and your mom live here alone, he sends you money but the dollar rate has increased so you're now living on ramen. Those are financial hardships.

In addition to these three types of hardships, if you are the first person in the family to go to college, it is also considered as a hardship. Especially in the United States, colleges like first generation college students and post the data  for admissions. Hardships are nothing to be ashamed about and they may help you get into college.

Now, you should not lie and make up stories of hardships. To be sure, chances are most of us may not have hardships. The biggest hardship that you may have is your TV remote control running out of batteries. That's not a hardship. But if you have a legitimate one, do write about it.

2) Who Are the Admissions Officers Reading Your Essays?

Let's profile a typical admissions officer – how old do you think he/she is?

Probably around 40 or 50. How much money do you think he or she gets paid? $100,000 a year? No way. The director of admissions may get paid that amount. According to Salary.com, an assistant admissions director gets paid on average $56,516 a year. Admissions officers travel part of the time to recruit students, but from November to April, they're reading hundreds of applications day after day at the office and at home. They are overworked, under-appreciated and exhausted people.

How much time does an admissions officer spend on your application? When I was working for the UC Berkeley undergraduate admissions office, I went to Berkeley two times a week and picked up 500 applications each time. So I went through 1,000 applications a week for six to eight weeks. If I have to go through 1,000 applications a week, how much time do you think I spend reading your essay? Two to three minutes tops. Therefore, you have to capture me within the first two or three minutes in your introductory paragraph— otherwise, it's just another ordinary essay about sports or music. Private universities will spend a little more time on the application. Nevertheless you have to have a powerful beginning to your essay. There is a reason the first sentence is called a hook. There were around 100 application readers at UC Berkeley when I was there. About 30% were African-American, about 25% were Hispanic, about 5% were Asian, and the rest were White. So, if you're gung-ho about your ethnicity, you may not be painting the most relatable picture of yourself. As my Harvard professor once told me, address the audience. The wrong way to grab this burdened reader is explaining a lofty topic without having anything personal to talk about.

Put yourself in the admissions officer's perspective— who do they want? What type of person, what kind of character? They want someone who understands and appreciate specific aspects of their college or university. This is particularly important when writing your supplements. You need to demonstrate why you are interested in that particular school. Topics such as beautiful campus, top-notch faculty, state-of-the-art facilities...you can say this about almost any top college in the U.S. Customize your essay for that particular college so when the admissions officer reads it, he or she is going to say, "Hey! This kid really is a good match for our school." You should not do this for the Common Application main essay though since the same essay will be sent to all the colleges you apply to.

91

3) Keys for A Successful College Essay

COLLEGE ESSAY

(A) Write from Your Soul

Write from your heart not from your head. Do not try to guess what admissions officers want to hear.

(B) Be Vivid and Precise

"My AP biology class was very hard so I had to study a long time for the exam." What's "very hard"? What's a "very long time"? These are relative terms. Everyone has a different definition. Whereas if you say "I stumbled out of bed at 5 o'clock every morning (my goodness, it's dark and this student is up at 5 am?! Wow!) for two years (whistle!) to shave hundredths of a second off my record in the 100 yard dash (hundredths of a second, I can visualize that).

(C) Never Write "Plethora" or "Epiphany"

While I was working as an admissions officer for UC Berkeley, we had a joke about "plethora" and "epiphany." It seems that many students want to write "plethora" and "epiphany." It's a cliché. Epiphany means what? Moment of discovering oneself. Say it in a different way. What's a plethora? Overwhelming number of, many, many, many. "I have a plethora of things to do in high school." And if you say, "Your expository is trivialized to metaphoric pedantry throughout your sycophant life," try again!

(D) Read Your Essay Out Loud

You should read your essay out loud. By reading your essay out loud, you will be able to see if it flows, makes sense, and sounds like you. Admissions officers are interested in hearing YOUR OWN VOICE. It is best to resist temptations to dazzle with gimmicks. They've seen it all. Presentation isn't going to get you further than the starting gate. Sincerity is what matters.

(E) Avoid Negative Words

Avoid words with negative connotations such as "never," "not," "don't," or "won't." "You *never* turn in your assignments late." NO! "You *always* turn your assignments in on time." What you're doing by writing these negative words is sending a subliminal message. By using negative words, you're saying, "No, I'm not going to get in," "Don't accept me," "I will never have a chance."

(F) Show Your Essay to Others

Show your essay to your English teacher, counselor, friends, and family members. Show your essay to at least three or four people who will read your essay objectively and subjectively to give their suggestions. You don't have to accept them all but at least get good feedback so it becomes a well-rounded, comprehensive essay. So no one may say, "It's a little biased—you're talking too much about your heritage or religion." Maybe you're talking too much about church and your commitment as a Christian. I read that a lot these days, and I want you to be careful. I'm a God-fearing, God-loving Christian too, but this essay is not about getting into seminary school. If you want to be a theology major and become a minister or priest it may work, but don't go all gung-ho about how much you're involved with church activities because this is not about going to heaven.

93

(G) Be In a Good Mood

Never write your college essay when you're tired or upset because your negativity comes out in your writing. The essays are due on November 1 for early decision. October comes around and your mom nags you to get started on your essay, "Hurry up, you're such a procrastinator!" You get into a big old fight, "Mom, I've been too busy! Alright! Alright! I'll do it!" So you start writing. It's not going to work. All that anger is going to come out in your essay. You have to be well rested and in a great mood. Remember, your cup is half full when you start drafting this college essay.

(H) Don't Go Off Topic

According to a former director of admissions at a top university, 85% of seniors who write their college essay do not answer the question. This is statistically proven. 85% of the applicants! For example, consider the essay question, "What was the most demanding event that occurred during your high school career?" Don't start off by saying, "When I was in elementary school…" When are we going to get to high school, by the end of the essay? Seven, eight, nine pages? They are asking *during high school.* So you should say something like, "When I was in 9th grade, 10th grade," not "When I was six years old." Yet students do this time after time, so be careful. When you write an essay, make sure you do not fall into the trap of saying what you want to say rather than what they ask you to say.

So what am I saying here? Say it from your heart, be passionate about what you're saying, pick a topic you're keenly aware of, think it through, paint a very clear and vivid picture, be concrete, don't mess around with prose, high vocabulary words, fancy letters, etc. Finally, be in a positive mindset when you write your college essays.

4) The Common Application Essay Questions

Most private schools use the Common Application. There are several different essay questions including a question of your own choice. These essay questions also represent the factors that colleges consider important. Top colleges have a few things in common. They look for intellectual vitality and diversity. Why? They want their alumni to go out and become influential leaders in society. They want their graduates to change the world for the better in various fields. They want someone who has challenged himself/herself beyond others, someone who has shown commitment, passion, and perseverance. They want someone who will overcome failures and look for solutions. They want someone who gives to others. Let's take a look at the essay questions and see how to answer them.

(A) Evaluate a significant experience, achievement, risk you have taken, or ethical dilemma you have faced and its impact on you.

What would be a good topic to talk about for this question? It could be something like, "In my AP class I noticed half a dozen kids started cheating—I could've easily joined the group, but I decided not to—so even though I got an A- in the class, I am proud of my achievement. I am proud of the fact that I maintained my virtues and high moral and ethical values." Not only should you talk in detail about the incident, but, more importantly, you need to clearly state what the impact was in a detailed manner. The answer should demonstrate what life lesson you learned from your experience. Harvard looks for students who make the most of their opportunities and the resources available to them, and who are likely to continue to do so throughout their lives. Yale says they look for someone who with Yale's help is likely to be a leader in whatever he or she ends up doing. Top colleges look for candidates with potential leadership, so use this essay to show how your leadership makes you stand out.

(B) Discuss some issue of personal, local, national, or international concern and its importance to you.

The environment, civil war, democracy, famine, gay rights, international piracy, nuclear proliferation... whatever topic shows your commitment and passion. You should stay away from controversial or extreme topics. Most top schools are fairly conservative. While creativity and thinking outside the box is great, you don't necessarily want to alarm the admissions officer. Be a maverick not an outlaw. As mentioned in the introduction to this chapter, top colleges want their alumni to care about the world and make a difference. Columbia selects applicants that will take the greatest advantage of the Columbia experience and offer something meaningful in return to the community. Dartmouth's president, Jim Yong Kim, suggests that Dartmouth looks for "passion and practicality... to tackle the challenges that we face today." You need to show the interest and the drive to impact the world.

(C) Indicate a person who has had a significant influence on you, and describe that influence.

Who is your role model? If it is your mom or your dad, why? Abraham Lincoln, why? Do not write a biography about the person, but the INFLUENCE ON YOU. Instead of just saying, "My mom worked hard," talk about the sacrifices in concrete terms, such as "She worked two jobs from 9 am to 9 pm six days a week to provide for us." By your word choice, you are showing who you admire and have as your role model. This essay will give the admissions officer a sense of your role as a member of society.

(D) Describe a character in fiction, a historical figure, or a creative work (as in art, music, science, etc.) that has had an influence on you, and explain that influence.

A character in a book, a historical figure—Mahatma Gandhi, Martin Luther King Jr., John F. Kennedy, Steve Jobs—whoever you felt has influenced you. Again, as in the previous essay question, you should make the essay about yourself not about the person. The influence is more important than the description. The answer to this essay will capture a similar idea as the essay question above.

(E) A range of academic interests, personal perspectives, and life experiences adds much to the educational mix. Given your personal background, describe an experience that illustrates what you would bring to the diversity in a college community or an encounter that demonstrated the importance of diversity to you.

This is all about diversity. Would you want all identical people at the university you attend? No. What can you bring? Brown seeks to create a mixture of individuals with different strengths and backgrounds that makes for the most dynamic and productive undergraduate community. For example, "During high school, I decided to have an international day by soliciting my Chinese, Korean, Persian, and Vietnamese friends. We brought together various ethnic food, dance and music. We helped teachers, staff, and students become aware of international cultures, AND I further plan to do this upon acceptance to the university, to broaden the world perspective on campus."

(F) Topic of your choice.

You pick the topic and answer it. Remember to stay away from extreme topics.

8. EXTRACURRICULAR ACTIVITIES

There are two phrases you should keep in mind for extracurricular activities: whether the activity shows either *leadership potential* or *special talent*. If it shows neither, you may be wasting your time.

For example, if you are a varsity member of the soccer team, does this demonstrate leadership talent? No, you're just a member. Does it demonstrate special talent? No. To be recognized as special talent, you need to be part of a state team, Olympic Junior team, or U.S. national team. Most students are not at that level. You may be good at playing the violin and the piano. However, during my 24 years of teaching I've come across only three students who have won awards at the national or international level in music. Nevertheless, if you do have talent, it is a plus. You may have a lower GPA and still get accepted. In 2008, five Korean female students from a soccer team in Irvine, California were accepted to Ivy League Schools. One was accepted to Harvard. They were members of an Irvine City Club Team, which won the State Championship. Their average SAT score was 1900 and their average GPA was 3.8. What? Yes! Harvard, Brown, and Princeton scouted these students because of their soccer talent. Now, let's not all go out and kick a soccer ball though.

Should you go to a leadership camp during the summer? Will it help your application? There are two issues to consider: does it show your leadership quality, and what is the size of the program? If it is for a small selective group of ten and you were selected from a large pool of applicants, then it is a worthwhile program. An example would be the Questbridge program. But if it's a leadership camp for 200 students, it won't have as much effect. It won't really help you get into college. Mission trips are the same. For example, if your church group is organizing a mission trip to Mexico, it's not going to help you to go to Mexico each year. However, you can do things to make a difference. You can plan your own project during the mission trip.

You need to make a decision at a certain point about your extracurricular activities. If you are exceptionally talented, then you should continue to develop that talent. However, if you are only competing at the school level, you need to focus on your studies more. There is not enough time. There are only twenty-four hours in a day, so you have to prioritize. Something has to give. There are very few students who do it all well: they are good at activities, get good grades and also get high SAT scores. Those kids only sleep three or four hours a night. Me, I like to sleep. I like to rest. I'm not one of those students who can function well with little sleep. Think about what you want to do.

Your extracurricular activities should show commitment and passion. They need to show you have spent your energy on meaningful activities that demonstrate a positive impact on other people; you have taken leadership roles when available and hold a deep appreciation for your activities. But remember you still have to allocate the majority of your time for studying.

9. LETTERS OF RECOMMENDATION

You may need one to three letters of recommendation to apply to top private colleges. All the letters have to be awesome. In other words, if you have one awesome letter of recommendation and one okay letter, this okay letter may get you rejected. How do you go about getting good letters? You have to sell yourself to your teacher now. Studying for school and SAT only will not cut it.

Number one, you have to smile and be nice to your teachers. It is silly to make them into your enemies because they are the ones who will write your recommendations. It doesn't matter if they are lousy teachers or you don't like them. Number two, befriend them! Go up to your teacher and say, "Hi, Mr. Johnson. Do you have anybody having a hard time in your class? I have some free time during lunch or after school. I'm willing to help." He's going to think, "Oh, Alex is not only a good student but he's willing to help less competent students." The teacher is going to remember that. "Hey, Mr. Johnson, I have a Christmas benefit concert coming up. I am going to raise money to buy food for homeless people. Would you like to come to the concert?" Your teacher is going to think, "Oh, Alex is not only a good student and willing to help less competent students, but he is also musically talented and raising money for homeless people." Number three, you need to keep promoting yourself so the teachers remember you. So when you ask for a recommendation, Mr. Johnson will remember all this and more when he starts typing your letter. Otherwise, what is he going to write? "Oh, he was a good student in my class." That's it. You need to stand out and be different from other students.

Let's say, out of 400 seniors in your high school, about 70 to 80 students want to go to top private colleges. So they need letters of recommendation. But, they're not only going to apply to one college, they're going to apply to five to ten colleges. So on average, five letters for 70 students is 350 letters. Who do you think these students are going to go to for their letters? Their favorite AP English, AP Calculus, or AP U.S. History teachers. So as a teacher, he or she has to write fifty to maybe one hundred letters. Now, the teachers don't get paid to write the letters. They have to do it in their private time at home or on the weekends. So unless they really like you, they are not going to spend a whole lot of time on the letter. They may have three different boiler plates: okay letters, good letters, and excellent letters. All they need to do is to just change the names and addresses. But, if they really like you, they are going to spend their time and write it up differently from the other kids. You need this type of outstanding letter. "Alex was one of the best students I've come across in my 24 years of teaching. He is not only gregarious but also a benevolent young man, who deeply cares about his classmates. He's always on time. He always does his assignments. He volunteers his time to help homeless people on weekends." You get the idea. That's what we have to do for Stanford, Ivy League schools, and other private schools that want letters of recommendation.

You should also think about what the evaluating categories are for the teacher evaluation in the Common Application. How would you evaluate yourself in each of these categories? What do you think your teacher will say about you? What areas do you need to improve on?

- Academic achievement
- Concern for others
- Creative, original thought

- Disciplined work habits
- Initiative, independence
- Integrity
- Intellectual promise
- Leadership
- Maturity
- Motivation
- Productive class discussion
- Quality of writing
- Reaction to setbacks
- Respect accorded by faculty
- Self-confidence

Here are some tips for requesting letters of recommendation written by the chairman of the English department at a college preparatory high school.

1) Do not ask more than one member of the department to write a recommendation for you, since no college requires more than one recommendation from a single subject teacher. This means if you get one recommendation from your AP U.S. History teacher, don't get the second recommendation from your AP European History teacher.

2) Request recommendations for only those schools to which you are definitely applying. Teachers are not given time by your high school's administration to write these letters. They take time out of their personal lives. The average length of time required to write a good letter ranges from one and a half to two hours.

3) Make certain that you allow at least one month (not counting vacation time) for the teacher to meet the deadline for your school. It will help if you supplement the teacher with a list of your colleges and their deadlines.

4) Make sure you have filled in your part of the application so that they do not have to find you to complete the information.

5) Remember that you are asking a teacher to do something for you. After a teacher has spent considerable time working on your behalf, you should take the trouble to tell that teacher, when the time comes, which school you finally selected.

6) Check back with the teacher in three or four weeks to ask them if they have any questions and gently remind them to get your recommendation out on time.

What steps should you take?

① Write a cover letter.

② Attach academic records and extracurricular activity lists.

③ Deliver the materials to the teacher.

④ Follow up three weeks later.

⑤ Write a thank you card NOT an email.

Here is a sample request for letters of recommendation:

REQUEST FOR RECOMMENDATION LETTER

Dear (Title and last name):

I really enjoyed your English class last year. I plan to apply to several private schools which require letters of recommendation: Cornell, Harvard, Princeton, and Stanford.

As my favorite teacher, I would kindly like to ask you to draft a letter by November 1st for Cornell, Harvard, Princeton, and Stanford. I am attaching a copy of my transcript and resume.

Thank you in advance for your prompt attention.

Sincerely,
(Your name and signature)

10. INTERVIEW

While the interview may not be the main deciding factor for getting accepted to college, if given the chance it is better to attend since it demonstrates your interest in the particular school. The interview is an important factor in the admissions decisions for MIT. On the MIT admissions website it states that interviews are strongly recommended. In fact, last year, of eligible applicants, MIT admitted 12.4% of those who had an interview (or who had their interview waived) but only 1.4% of those who chose not to interview. Also the Ivy League schools all take the interview into consideration when making admissions decision; therefore, you better do well or else you're not going to get in. Interviews are done one on one by alumni. It takes about 30 minutes to one hour.

Interview Tips

1. Take a copy of your resume or pre-interview form to help you organize.
2. Dress conservatively but not too formally.
3. Arrive 5 minutes before the interview time.
4. Make direct eye contact with the interviewer.
5. Give a firm handshake rather than a wimpy one.
6. Smile and be polite.
7. Answer in full sentences but do not be long winded.
8. Prepare some questions about the school to ask the interviewer.
9. Send a thank you email after the interview.

"I would say that in preparing for admissions to college or graduate school, an applicant should develop a history of demonstrated leadership and excellence in his or her field of interest. Pick activities and academic subjects that you can shine in and that go above and beyond the common features that define a high school student or college student. Quality over quantity: for example, instead of spending volunteer hours at a soup kitchen, create a project that tackles issues of hunger and aid on a local or international level. Begin to publish your writing if you aspire to be a writer. Collaborate on research at a university if you are interested in science. Bring your skills and knowledge to an underdeveloped community. You need to start thinking about how you fit into society and can contribute to a greater cause, whether that is academic, service, or business related. Take your interests and passions and focus them through the lens of these leadership roles. People who work outside of the box and demonstrate their value on their own terms are sought after in all fields. And from these accomplishments and life experiences, you will be able to reflect on who you are, what you want to achieve, and how your resume has prepared you for these goals. That is ultimately what makes an essay and application of any kind worth reading."

Alex Rosenberg, Cornell, Class of 2010
(former Ivy Review student)

PART III

COLLEGE APPLICATION PROCESS

1. COLLEGE APPLICATION PLANNING

Preparing your college applications is a hectic process. Don't leave everything until the last minute. I have heard of cases where acceptances get revoked because of missing documents. Below is a month-by-month list of the things you need to do to prepare your applications during your senior year.

AUGUST

- ☑ List your top college choices.
- ☑ Request admissions information and school catalogs.
- ☑ Go on college visits.
- ☑ Decide on early or regular admissions.
- ☑ Register online for the Common Application.

SEPTEMBER

- ☑ If you haven't already taken the SAT and/or ACT, register for the test(s).
- ☑ Ask employers, teachers, and guidance counselors for letters of recommendation to accompany your applications.

OCTOBER

- ☑ Register for/take the SAT and/or ACT.
- ☑ Work on your college essays.
- ☑ Attend college planning and/or financial aid information nights and college fairs.
- ☑ Complete applications for scholarships.
- ☑ Finalize portfolios, audition tapes, writing samples, or other evidence of talent if required for admissions.

NOVEMBER

☑ Complete admission applications by their deadlines. Early Decision is November 1. UC is November 30.

☑ If necessary, register to retake the SAT and/or ACT. This is the last test you can submit to UC.

☑ Request financial aid forms and applications.

☑ Follow up on letters of recommendation.

DECEMBER

☑ Third time's a charm. Register to retake the SAT and/or ACT if necessary.

☑ Finalize admission applications.

☑ Research and apply for other financial aid, including grants and scholarships.

☑ Watch for early admission notices.

JANUARY

☑ Complete your FAFSA online.

FEBRUARY

☑ Be mindful of deadlines. Always submit information on time.

☑ Review your Student Aid Report (SAR) for errors and make any corrections as indicated.

☑ Send your mid-year high school grade report to colleges. Your counselor can help.

MARCH

- ☑ Check with the financial aid offices to ensure your paperwork is complete.

- ☑ Be on the lookout for acceptance letters.

- ☑ Register for Advanced Placement (AP) exams.

APRIL

- ☑ Compare financial aid award letters.

- ☑ Make your final school decision and mail deposits, as required.

- ☑ Notify the schools you have chosen NOT to attend.

- ☑ Plan for registration, orientation, and housing, and mark your calendar with important dates.

MAY

- ☑ Make plans for summer orientation sessions.

- ☑ Follow up with your high school to ensure your final school transcripts have been sent to the college.

2. EARLY OR REGULAR?

Because the admit rate is noticeably higher for early admissions compared to regular admissions, you may consider applying early to the top school of your choice. You need to be aware that the higher admit rate does not mean that it will be easier to get in. There are a few things to consider.

First, are you all set to apply for the early round? This means that your academic courses, SAT/ACT, and extracurricular activities should all be completed before November 1. If you plan to apply early, it is not a good idea to wait and take the SAT/ACT in October because you will have to wait until your scores come out before making your final school choice. What this does to you is that instead of preparing your essays and supplements, you put them aside and waste valuable time. Therefore, if you plan to apply early, then prepare early.

Class of 2016 Admissions						
Colleges	Early Decisions			Regular Decisions		
	Applied	Accepted	Admit Rate	Applied	Accepted	Admit Rate
Brown	2,919	556	19.0%	25,823	2,204	8.5%
Columbia	3,088	631	20.4%	28,730	1,732	6.0%
Cornell	3,609	1,180	32.7%	34,203	4,943	14.5%
Dartmouth	1,801	465	27.5%	21,309	1,715	8.0%
Harvard	4,245	772	18.2%	30,057	1,260	4.2%
MIT	6,008	680	11.3%	12,101	940	7.8%
Princeton	3,547	726	20.5%	23,221	1,369	5.9%
Stanford	5,880	755	12.8%	30,751	1,772	5.8%
U Penn	4,526	1,148	25.4%	26,690	2,698	10.1%
Yale	4,310	675	15.7%	24,664	1,300	5.3%

Second, if you get rejected in the early round, you will have to give up on that college. You might have a better chance if you apply during the regular round so you need to know strategically when the best time is for you personally to apply. If you get rejected in the early round, you may not apply to the same school during the regular round. Remember, a student may apply early decision to only one institution. Therefore, if an early decision applicant applies for early decision to more than one school, the early decision applications will be withdrawn by all the schools. Also, if any regular decision applicant is accepted early decision by another school, the regular decision applications will be withdrawn.

Each school may have a different policy regarding the early round. Here is a list for the Ivy League and other top universities and their policies:

- Binding Early Decision

  If admitted, ED applicants must withdraw their applications from other colleges and agree to enroll.

- Single Choice Early Action

  You may not apply to an early program at any other private college or university, but you may apply early to any public institution, as long as the decision is nonbinding.

- Early Action / Restrictive Early Action

  This is a non-binding admission option and admitted students have until May 1 to respond to their admission offer.

- Non-Binding Early Action

  If accepted in the early round, students have until December 20 to respond to their admissions offer.

College	Policy[5]
Brown	Binding Early Decision
CalTech	Early Action
Columbia	Binding Early Decision
Cornell	Binding Early Decision
Dartmouth	Binding Early Decision
Harvard	Single Choice Early Action
MIT	Early Action
Princeton	Single Choice Early Action
Stanford	Restrictive Early Action
U Penn	Non-Binding Early Decision
Yale	Single Choice Early Action

[5] As of 2011-12 Academic Year.

"When it comes to gaining admission to the college or your choice, never underestimate the power of planning ahead. In this increasingly competitive college admissions landscape, it is imperative that an applicant distinguishes him/herself through consistent and purposeful leadership in and outside of the classroom. Strong grades are more common than you think. You must impress the admission committee with initiative and passion. For example, my high school career was marked by a presidency of 3 different organizations in addition to substantial volunteer work in my community. My classmates had similar track records. If you think intensively about how you can get more involved, you will inevitably be on the track to college admission success. This preparation coupled with a sound strategy should help you compete with the cream of the crop. Be excited for your future acceptance letters."

Anonymous, Harvard, Class of 2011

3. THE COMMON APPLICATION

The Common Application is used for applicants to apply to the 456 colleges that are members of the Common App as of 2011. It provides a standardized application form for first year (freshman) and transfer applicants. The application and all relevant supplements should be submitted online unless indicated otherwise. The Common Application consists of the following:

www.commonapp.org

1) Applicant Information

This section includes the basic information of the applicant such as name, date of birth, address, phone number, and email. If you go by several names, use the name that is on your high school transcript. If you have changed your name legally, you can add information about this in the "additional information" section in the writing section. For your college applications, I strongly recommend that you create an email account that represents your name. Nicknames, game characters, or any suggestive phrases are not appropriate. For example, do not use megamanbass, stupidlisa, or whiskeylove to communicate with admissions officers.

2) Future Plans

One of my students asked me, "Do I randomly choose colleges for future plans?" ABSOLUTELY NOT! By the time you start the application process, you should have a clear idea of what colleges you want to apply to, public or private, early or regular decision. Your intended major and career choice will give the colleges an idea of what your focus will be once you get into college. They will evaluate your application to see if you have demonstrated commitment and passion for it. You may or may not indicate your desired major. Sometimes, it is strategically better to choose an easier major for admissions purposes. However, you will need to see whether you will be able to change majors once you get into the college. Some majors such as engineering may be different, so do your research beforehand.

3) Demographics

Get all your demographic information correct. The best way to prepare for your application is to download the paper form and fill it out first with a pencil. Ask your parents and counselor all the questions before you start filling out your application. Is it better to indicate your ethnicity? Again, this will depend on the school and major you wish to apply to. In my opinion, it is difficult not to conclude that some elite universities do indeed impose a quota—at least unofficially or subconsciously. Princeton sociologist Thomas J. Espenshade disclosed in his article, "Evaluative Judgments vs. Bias in College Admissions," that when comparing applicants with similar grades, scores, athletic qualifications, and family history for seven elite private colleges and universities: Whites were three times as likely to get accepted as Asians, Hispanics were twice as likely to win admission as Whites, and African-Americans were at least five times as likely to be accepted as Whites.

4) Family

Again, get accurate information from your parents. If your parents went to college or graduate school in a foreign country, get the correct spelling of the official name of their schools, year of graduation, and degree. The best way to get the official name of your parents' colleges is to check the websites of the colleges they graduated from. If your parents did not attend college, this is actually a good thing so don't be discouraged! Many colleges seek to give opportunities to first generation college students and provide such data in their freshmen profiles.

Depending on your situation, you may or may not be living with both parents. There are also sensitive family issues to consider here. Let's say, your parents got divorced and your mother, who has full custody, got remarried and you are now living with your stepfather. Then, whose information do you put in the "father" section— your biological father or your stepfather? This would depend on whether your stepfather has adopted you legally. So again, check with your parents to get accurate information.

5) Education

Secondary school is defined as the high school that you are attending. If you have attended several high schools because you moved or attended a summer program at another high school, don't forget to include that information. This will also include online high school courses taken at other institutes. For colleges and universities, be sure to include the summer programs and community colleges you attended as well. You should also list enrichment programs hosted on college campuses and online college courses. Include the titles of courses taken and grades earned in the Additional Information area of the Writing section. If you received a transcript from an accredited college or university that indicates college credit earned at that institution make sure to check the "Yes" box and send the official transcript as soon as possible.

6) Academics

(A) Grades

While this section is optional, it is always better to report this information if your numbers are impressive.
- Class rank and weighting
- Graduating class size
- Cumulative GPA score, scale, and weighting

This information is usually on your high school transcript. If not, go to your counselor and ask. The Common Application does not require you to submit the grading system for your high school. Your counselor will submit the school reports for this.

(B) Standardized Test Scores

I sometimes find it amazing that students do not know where to get their test scores.

- SAT and SAT II: http://www.collegeboard.org
- ACT: http://www.actstudent.org
- AP Exams: 888 308-0013
- TOEFL: http://www.ets.org/toefl/
- IELTS: http://www.ielts.org

You will need to include ALL the test dates, and/or the best scores (super scores) for each section depending on the college policy. If you take the tests in November or December, remember to update your test information before you submit your application.

(C) Current Year Courses

These are the courses you will be taking during your senior year. Each year, the new version of the Common Application comes out in August. You may not be able to get an accurate course schedule for your senior year until school starts in the fall. So, remember to update this information once your courses are finalized. Make sure to put in the correct course title, level (Honors, AP, or IB), and number of credits. Many students forget to put in the number of credits for each course. Each high school has a different system; some high schools say one course is 5 credits, others will indicate it as 0.5 credits. So use what is on your transcript.

7) Honors and Awards

In this section, you will list the academic awards you have received SINCE 9TH GRADE. This includes academic certificates, medals, trophies, and scholarships you may have received. For example, AP Scholar with Distinction Award

or Outstanding Achievement Recognition by your school or district would be something you would list here. Although you may have awards from 6th, 7th, or 8th grade, there is no place to indicate them on the Common Application. In addition, any non-academic awards should not be listed in this section. For example, first place in an international dance competition should not be listed here. However, you can list this award in the next section, Activities.

8) Activities

Your extracurricular activities should be listed in the order of importance. You will be able to add up to ten activities in this section. Any others that you cannot report here can be added in the "Additional Information" of the Writing Section. The activities are usually categorized into the following types

Academic	Family Responsibilities
Art	Foreign Exchange
Athletic	Foreign Language
Career Oriented	Journalism
Community Service	Music
Computer/Technology	Religious
Cultural	Science/Math
Dance	Student Government
Debate/Speech	Theater/Drama
Environmental	Others

Paid and unpaid work, volunteering, sports, musical instruments, science clubs are some of the activities you can list here. In fewer than 60 characters, you will need to succinctly describe the details and accomplishments of your activity. You also need to describe the position held, honors received, letters earned, or employment title. Therefore, it is crucial to choose each word wisely to best describe the activity in a way that will set your application apart from others. It is far better to record the top five or six activities rather than list mundane activities to fill out all ten slots. In addition, if the activity is something you plan to continue in college, the admissions officers will look at it more closely as it is a good indicator of what you can contribute to the college community. So remember to click on the box that says, "I intend to participate while in college."

9) Writing

The first essay you will write is a short essay on one of your extracurricular activities or work experiences in 1,000 characters. Since you will already have listed this activity in your activity list, it will be better to add new information that will give insight into your activity, such as an interesting anecdote that shows what you learned and what you will do in the future.

For the main essay, you will choose one of the six questions and write an essay between 250 and 500 words. The Common Application essay does not have a maximum word limit, but it should be approximately 2 pages single-spaced. Remember, quality over quantity! In addition to the Common Application essay, you may have to write supplemental essays for each college that you apply to. Since the Common Application essay will be sent to all the colleges that you apply to, it should not be customized for one specific college; however, you can customize the supplemental essays for each college.

10) Additional Information

Here is the place to add any information that you were unable to put elsewhere in the application. This is also a good place to make yourself stand apart from other applicants. The Common Application is limited and you may not be able to include all the information that shows your strengths. So use this space wisely. Now, don't go crazy and add too many pages. Limit this section to two or three pages maximum. You can add any type of information that will strengthen your application such as:

- Additional AP or SAT Subject Test scores

- Explanation of major ups and downs in grades

- Any special circumstances that were not explained in the application such as family problems or hardships

- Any other activities or awards that were not included in the Activity section

A word of caution before you hit the "submit" button. Some text may be cut off when your application is printed. Not all content that 'fit' on the online application will 'fit' on the PDF of the Common Application. Why? Who knows? While the answers you provide on the online application are within the character limit for a given field, it is possible that those answers may be cut off when the PDF of your Common Application is generated. If you preview the Common App and find some of your text is missing, you should attempt to shorten your response to fit within the available space. While colleges are aware of this issue, it is up to you to make sure your application is flawless.

"Getting into a top college is certainly a four-year effort, but it is also crucial that you put together a stellar application. The admissions officers will see what you have done throughout high school, so grades, course load difficulty, extracurricular involvement and leadership are all important factors. But if you did not excel in most or all of these areas, you can still boost your chances of getting accepted by drafting a thoughtful personal statement and supplemental essays, if applicable. I spent a lot of time refining my supplemental essays for Stanford's application, which I think helped the admissions officers hear my voice and see what I could contribute to the Stanford community. Taking the time to create a polished application can turn a potential rejection into an acceptance, so make sure you take advantage of this last opportunity to impress the admissions officers."

Anonymous, Stanford, Class of 2011

PART IV

CONCLUSION

1. TO THE STUDENTS

In the 2011-2012 academic year, the UC Berkeley fall freshman average high school GPA was 4.14, and the average SAT was 2073.[6] The SAT scores of the middle 50% of the students accepted to Princeton as freshmen in 2011 had a critical reading score between 700 and 790, math score between 710 and 800, and a writing score between 700 and 790.[7] 21.6% of the Princeton freshmen of 2011 received an SAT score between 2300 - 2400. I'm not trying to depress you or make you scared. These are the facts. I didn't make this up. This is a reality check.

Sophomores, this is the year where everything counts. Juniors, you are almost done with school work and will have an idea of where you can get into. So apply yourself a little more and you can get into a better college. Now, in case you didn't know all this and you're a senior, don't despair. Don't go, "Had I known all this stuff I would have done so much better. I should have read this book sooner." It's not the end of your future. It's ok. Don't give up. There is nothing we can do about the past. However, there is always something you can do about the future. For example, just do your best to improve your GPA and apply to the best colleges you can, wherever that may be. Then really work hard during the first year. Don't slack off and regret again. After the first year, you can always transfer to a better school, let's say Stanford, and in four years you will have a Stanford diploma hanging on your wall. If you maintain an excellent academic performance in college, this is possible.

---

[6]   http://www.universityofcalifornia.edu/admissions/campuses/berkeley/
       freshman-profile/index.htm
[7]   Princeton Profile 2011-2012, www.princeton.edu/admission

What if transferring doesn't work? Then, there is always graduate school. For liberal arts majors, graduating from college may not be enough these days. So many of these students go on to graduate schools to get an MBA, PHD, MD, or JD. So for undergraduate work, do the best you can, then go to a top graduate school. If you didn't get into Harvard College, work hard and go to Harvard Law School or Harvard Medical School. Ultimately, what matters the most is what you have accomplished in life and how much positive difference you have made in this world.

The bottom line is to do the best you can with the circumstances that you have right now. Not everyone who reads this book is going to go to Harvard. Not everyone can go to Stanford or UC Berkeley. And you know what? That's ok. I don't want you to stress over that right now. It's not the end of the world. But we should try to do the best we can with our God-given talent. Why waste it? Don't waste time on Facebook, games, texting, or TV especially in 10th and 11th grade, when these are such important periods in your life. If you wasted your time yesterday, don't anymore.

Starting today, stop, because you are being silly. You are the one going to college. It is not your mom or dad. They're done. This is about your life. From now on, it should not be mom and dad trying to push you to study or do your homework anymore. You have to say, "I have to want to do this, because this is my life. I'm going to screw up my life if I keep this up." You have to realize that. And the sooner you realize this, the easier it is going to be on you in high school, college, and the rest of your life.

What I'm saying is that you need to be independent. For example, from now, don't let your mom wake you up for school. You get up late for school? You're going to be tardy. You're late once? Twice, three times? Finally, you're going to think, "I'm in trouble. I need to get up early from now on. I better go to bed early." You will set one, two, three, four even five alarm clocks if need be to get up early the next day. You may put a bucket of cold water above your head. Just kidding! You need to build your independence. Otherwise, you are not going to make it through the first semester of college and may even get expelled. I've seen it happen to many top high school students. These students were excellent students in high school. Then, they get into college, without the supervision of their parents, and they screw up. Don't get dependent on your mom or dad to make the responsible decisions for you.

For example, did you know that many college students are in credit card debt today? What happens? They run out of money. So, what do they do? Many of these kids have credit card debt because  of uncontrolled spending habits. If you go to college, you get tons of credit card applications. All you need to do is to put in your social security number, address, phone number, email, and name, and voilà! The company gives you a credit card! You don't care if the interest rate is really high. You don't tell your mom and dad that you got a credit card. You get another credit card. Spend it. Debt starts to pile up. I even had friends declare bankruptcy at the age of twenty-one.

Independence is the right action to take. Ask yourself what is important for you in school? What happens if you don't study? Independence is not getting upset because mom or dad nags you to study. You want mom or dad to leave you alone? Then, you have to be responsible for taking care of your own business.

Why would mom and dad tell you to study if you're doing it? He or she is on your back because you're NOT doing it!

If you get straight As and get a 2400 on the SAT, your parents wouldn't care if you are on Facebook. It's because you didn't do your job. It's because you could have done better. That's why mom and dad are involved. They know their son. They know their daughter. They know he or she could do better than this.

INVEST THE TIME!
MAKE THE SACRIFICES!
SET YOUR PRIORITIES!

Your parents work hard for your future in the United States. They're making sacrifices. For what? FOR YOU GUYS! Now, if you're the oldest, your parents expect more. Why? Because your younger brother or sister is watching you. Your younger siblings may pretend like they don't care, but they're watching you and will soon imitate you. So if you do well, they're going to do well. They'll watch you and imitate you. How do I know? Because I'm the oldest. I have two younger brothers. I didn't grow up in a nice neighborhood. I grew up in a very high crime area. We had gangs. We had drugs. I could have joined a gang. I could have used drugs. I never did. Because in my head, I saw my parents, risking their lives, working seven days a week, fourteen hours a day in a convenience store. My parents were robbed at gunpoint twice. If I think about that, how could I even consider doing drugs, slacking off or joining a gang? I wanted to study because I knew my parents were risking their lives for me and my brothers every day. I did well, and so did my brothers. All three of us went to Harvard. If I could come to the U.S. as an eleven year old and go to Harvard, so can you!

I know many of you were born in the U.S. So you are much better off than I was. When I was growing up, I didn't go to SAT prep. I didn't have books like this. But you? Here, I just gave you the blueprint. I just gave you the road map for getting into the top colleges in the U.S. You are so much better off than I was. You have a much better chance than I ever had. Do well. For yourself! For your parents. Don't compare yourself with other kids out there. Who cares? Be yourself! Be yourself and see what is best for you and what can you do for your future. So you better be in the mind set to study from now on.

My parents worked really hard for 25 years and now they're retired. They're 75 and 74 today. They live in California. I bought them a house. My brother bought them a car. They play golf five days a week, enjoying their retirement. Why am I telling you this? Don't you want this for your dad? Don't you want this for your mom? They are working so hard for you right now! If you do well, you can help them out financially. Your parents don't have to pay for your tuition. Wouldn't that be nice? Let the government and corporations pay for your education! During my four years of college, I received a full scholarship. My parents did not have to pay one penny for my college education. I went to the financial aid office and the cashier would give me a check every quarter. I used that money to buy books, computers, and furniture. In fact, I still have the desk that I bought in college with the scholarship money at my Dublin office.

You can do it too. All you have to do is spend more time. You want those good grades? You want that perfect SAT score? Just spend more time. Start today. Do it now!

2. TO THE PARENTS

1) Positive Reinforcement

Please give your child lots of positive reinforcement. You should build up their confidence. Praise them at least once a day. Find one thing about your child and praise them. "Your hair looks really nice today, my handsome." "You got up so early today, princess. I am so proud of you!" Going to school with this compared to, "Hey! You're late again! I can't believe you! You do this every day!" What a big difference!

Pause and think about it before you get angry. Why did my kid get a C? Instead of yelling at him, why don't you say, "How can I help you?" He feels guilty already. He feels bad. If you put him down more, where is he going to stand? He may even run away. He could do drugs, drink, hang out with the wrong friends, smoke, or even worse. I have seen this happen. You need to give your children loving care. Then, they will do better by themselves. They will know what to do better next time. I'll give you an example. A few years ago in LA, after five weeks we gave a diagnostic test, and two students, Frank and Aaron, improved identically +100 points. Frank told his mother and she said, "I can't believe you! You call this studying?! I just got off the phone with Jane's mom. She said Jane's score went up 120 points!" Think about this. Do you think Frank tries harder next time? He is probably thinking, "My mom is never going to be happy, never going to be satisfied. Forget it." He doesn't try. Why should he since he only got scolded?

Aaron improved 100 points too just as Frank. But when Aaron went to his mom, she said, "Aaron! Good job! I'm so proud of you. You worked so hard. Let's go out and celebrate. What do you want for lunch? How about some dim sum?" Aaron is thinking, "Yes! Mom praised me. She wants to take me out to lunch. Cool! You know what? I'm going to try even harder next time." Let's say Aaron's score went down. What would his mom say? "It's all right, Aaron. You must not be in a good condition today. Forget about it. It's not even a real test; it's just a practice test. Next time, if you work hard, I'm sure your score will go up. Let's forget about it and grab something good to eat. How about some dim sum?" Aaron wasn't scolded. His mom is encouraging him, trying to help. I am sure Aaron is going, "Yes, she's right. I can do it. I'm going to try harder."

When I see students in my class, I know how their parents treat them at home. You may have been like that yesterday, but please change starting today. These kids are American teenagers. They don't get yelled at in school. Look at their teacher in school. What is the first thing the teacher says when you go to a conference? He or she always starts with the good behavior, praising the student. "Alex is such a good student. He always comes to class on time." Then what comes next? "But." There is always that infamous "but"; it's an American custom. There is a saying, "Praise in public. Punish in private." Don't yell at your kids in front of their friends. How would that make them feel? I know it's hard as a parent. Sometimes, you just want to blow up whether or not their friends are watching but you've got to keep it cool. Why? Because you don't want to scar them for life.

2) Provide Unconditional Love

Parents I need your help. You have to give your children unconditional love. Unconditional love doesn't mean if you get straight As, I'll buy you a new BMW. That's conditional love. No matter what they do, even if they are a straight

131

F student, you need to love them the same. That's unconditional love. Why? Because they are your children. They may be big physically, but in their minds, in their hearts, they are still growing. When they go to school, they face a lot of pressure. They get pressure from other kids that you know— friends, relatives, and siblings. And what is the one thing students hate the most? When they are being compared with another student. They hate that. I know it's hard for parents, because I do that too sometimes. But try to limit comparing, try to minimize that urge as much as you can and understand your children's perspectives.

Dads, I know that it can be difficult for dads to express affection, especially to your sons. There are fathers who have never hugged their kids, who have never said, "I love you" to their own kids. There are so many kids like this today. These kids go to their friend's house or watch TV and see how affectionate other parents are. "I love you dad, I love you mom." Kissing. But your child is deprived of that. If it's too awkward, then write him a little note. "Ted, I'm so proud of you. You've done so well in the last quarter, I am proud to be your dad." Put it in their lunch bag or backpack. Think how happy your son will be when he reads your love note.

3) Teach Independence

Starting tomorrow, please do not wake up your son or daughter to go to school on time. If he gets up late for school, let him be tardy. Don't wake him up. I mean it! Let him be late once? Twice? Three times? Leave him alone until he says, "I'm in trouble. I need to get up early from now on. I better go to bed early and stop staying up late playing games and Facebooking my friends." He will set one, two alarm clocks to get up early the next day. You need to help him build his own independence. Otherwise, he's not going to make it through college and life.

I've seen it happen. Students who were top students in high school get into top colleges. Then, without the supervision of the parents, they do not succeed. Your children need to have the strength to stand on their own two feet and the independence to do what is important for them in school now, throughout the week and year. Don't tell them to study anymore. Have you tried reverse psychology? Try asking them to do the opposite of what you want them to do. You know your daughter or son better than anyone else in the world. You know he or she can do better than this. In the end, you are sacrificing and working for what? For your son or daughter! Right? May God bless you and your family! Please take my advice to heart. Thank you for reading my book!